Memories

of

Croydon

Part of the

Memories

series

The Publishers would like to thank the following companies for supporting the production of this book

Main Sponsor
The Whitgift Shopping Centre

Allders

The Dove Group

Francis, Townsend & Hayward

HR Jennings & Company Limited

Landis & Gyr Communications (UK) Limited

OCS Group Limited

Paynes

Philips Electronics

Rawling & Son

The House of Reeves

Rowland Brothers

Selsdon Park Hotel

Tramtrack Croydon Limited

Zotefoams plc

First published in Great Britain by True North Books Limited
West Yorkshire HX3 6AE
Tel. 01422 344344
© Copyright: True North Books Limited 1999
This edition reprinted in paperback, 2002

ISBN 1 903204 67 4

Text, design and origination by True North Books Limited
Printed and bound in Great Britain

Memories are made of this

Memories. We all have them; some good, some bad, but our memories of the town we grew up in are usually tucked away in a very special place in our minds. The best are usually connected with our childhood and youth, when we longed to be grown up and paid no attention to adults who told us to enjoy being young, as these were the best years of our lives. We look back now and realise that they were right.

So many memories - perhaps of the war and rationing, perhaps of parades, celebrations and Royal visits. And so many changes; one-way traffic systems and pedestrianisation.

New trends in shopping that led to the very first self-serve stores being opened.

Through the bad times and the good, however, Croydon not only survived but prospered. We have only to look at the town as it is today, with its finest buildings restored to their full glory, and the traditional tourist attractions now complemented by up-to-the-minute facilities, to see what progress has been realised and what achievements have been made over the last 50 years. Croydon has a history to be proud of - but more importantly, a great future to look forward to, into the new millennium and beyond.

Contents

Section one
Around the town centre

•

Section two
At leisure

•

Section three
Events & occasions

•

Section four
Wartime

•

Section five
On the move

•

Section six
Shopping spree

•

Section seven
At work

Around the town centre

Croydon Local Studies Library

The mid-calf hemlines, neat little hats and shopping bags help us to identify this as a scene from the 1950s; trilby hats were still fashionable wear for men at the time, though times were about to change even in the gents' department. Note the short trousers and knee length socks worn by the small boy on the left. The only time you would get your son into shorts today would probably be on his summer holidays in Benidorm! This rather gallant youngster is helping his mum by carrying her parcels, nicely wrapped, you will notice, in brown paper and tied securely with string - a far cry from the plastic carriers of today, which clutter our streets and fasten themselves to the branches of trees.

Crossing the road could be a problem even in the 1950s, when post-war prosperity was beginning to be felt and more people were able to afford a family car. Here, a police officer has been drafted in to help pedestrians cross near the old Public Hall in George Street.

Croydon's magnificent red brick Town Hall, clock tower and public library draw the eye in this pigeon's eye view of the town as it was in 1927. The view will be an unfamiliar one to younger readers whose memories of Croydon are limited to the town since it was modernised; today of course the Flyover bisects the scene from left to right. A sharp eye will perhaps spot the open top trams in High Street; imagine how wet and uncomfortable they would be on rainy days! The tram drivers were even worse off than the passengers, as trams had no windscreens until the late 1930s. They were provided with leather aprons as protection from the weather, but we can imagine what a comfortless job tram driving would have been in a harsh winter! The Town Hall and library complex was opened in 1896. The facility was extended in the early 1990s, the new parts, designed by architects Tibbalds Monro, blending tastefully with the Victorian building. Few Croydonians will not have experienced for themselves the superb new library, arts centre, museum and cafe, while the Tourist Information Centre is convenient for visitors to the town.

The John Gent Collection

By kind permission of the Croydon Advertiser Group

Above: This marvellously evocative scene in High Street dates from the late 1940s, and the street simply buzzes with life - as the same spot still does today. The Davis Theatre was open at the time, and the Green Dragon pub stood almost opposite - handy for a quick nightcap to round off an evening's entertainment! Croydon once had a wealth of ancient hostelries, and The Green Dragon was one of them. The historic inn was opened in High Street a couple of years after the great fire of London, at a time when Isaac Newton was building his reflecting telescope, and van Leeuwenhoek was making his observations of red blood corpuscles. The Green Dragon was to suffer the same fate as the Davis Theatre; both were demolished around 1960 and were replaced by modern office blocks. High Street was well known in Croydon for the entertainment it offered, with the Davis Theatre, the Palladium and the Grand Theatre situated within a stone's throw of each other.

Above right: Traffic was heavy in High Street when this busy scene was caught on camera. The year was 1939, and wartime petrol rationing, introduced on 22nd September that year, would soon make a difference in the level of traffic as motor car owners queued with the rest for public transport. The driver of the racy motor on the left was making the best of the summer sunshine - and perhaps posing a little for the benefit of the girls at the same time? The fine Post Office building, quite remarkably, is still a very busy branch of the Post

Office more than 60 years on. Having escaped the red pen of the planners and survived road widening and redevelopment schemes, it is today sandwiched between the Bar Monaco and Rawlings Opticians. Note the lone cycle that has been parked at the kerb while its owner pops in for a penny stamp; those were the gentler days when you could go off and do your shopping, and expect to find your bike still there when you got back.

This wonderful view of the junction of Crown Hill, George Street and North End dates from the 1930s, and gives us a revealing glimpse back through time to the way things used to be. From our perspective 60 or so years on, the roads do not appear to be very busy, yet the authorities have thought it necessary to place a police officer on point duty. If the car turning towards us from George Street is intending to go down Crown Hill, the smart black saloon stationed slightly to the right of the crown of the road has left him precious little room to manoeuvre. Will the driver's thoughtlessness

merit a stern word or two from the bobby, we wonder? At least we can be reasonably certain that neither will be a victim of road rage....

The advertisements in the foreground add interest to the scene; Yardley's Lavender toilet water was a firm favourite with ladies at the time, and the forthcoming attractions at the Empire inform us that August is upon us - and that the year is 1935. Readers should note the cobbled roadway far below; think of the enormous amount of manpower needed to place each one of those granite setts!

Right: How many of our younger readers have identified this scene as Park Lane? The same view today has changed so much as to be almost unrecognisable. Today, St George's House, the 260ft high 23-storey headquarters of the giants Nestle, dominates the right of the scene, while the underpass and Croydon Technical College now lie to the left. Traffic was already becoming a problem when this photograph was taken in 1956, even though far fewer families owned a car. Most people still travelled by public transport, a fact which is borne out by the number of buses in this shot. Buses had long been regarded as convenient mobile advertising hoardings, and the Number 194 in the foreground, bound for Shirley, carries twin adverts for Biro, 'The original ball point pen'. Ball point pens, taken so much for granted today, had only been around for 12 years at the time of the photograph. Invented by Hungarian Laszlo Biro, the new pens quickly caught on and eventually made themselves indispensable around the world.

By kind permission of the Croydon Advertiser Group

Below: The parish church clock informs us that the time is 9.35am, and road works are in progress in Church Street, presenting a potential obstruction to traffic...so what's new? The only thing missing from the scene is a set of temporary traffic lights! St Johns is a church with a very long history, as a place of worship existed on this site as long ago as the year 871. The medieval church survived until the winter of 1867, when fire swept through the building, destroying most of its historic memorials including that of Archbishop Sheldon. The Archbishop's spirit, so the story goes, could not rest and haunted the burnt out ruins until the church and its tombs were rebuilt. Sir Gilbert Scott designed the new church, which was slightly larger than the older building, making it the largest church in Surrey. The parish church is the last resting place of no fewer than six Archbishops of Canterbury, including John Whitgift, who died in 1604.

Yet more history lies to the right of the photograph, which was taken in the 1950s. The Rose and Crown pub still possesses some of its Victorian tiling and stained glass, though parts of the old inn are around 300 years old.

The John Gent Collection

Judging by the number of pedestrians in George Street, each one walking purposefully, this photograph would appear to capture Croydon in the rush hour. The scene communicates an urgency that tells us that this is the end of a long hard day in the office or the shop. A nice cup of tea, a hot meal, and perhaps the added attraction of an evening spent in the pub, is the thought that is uppermost in the minds of all these workers. Looking in the direction of East Croydon Street and the railway station from the corner of Wellesley Road, the view takes in the grocery warehouse of John Thrift's and its impressive clock tower. Interestingly, the clock had originally belonged to Croydon's second Town Hall, which was demolished in 1893. The tower together with all the properties on the left were demolished in the road widening schemes that transformed the town during the 1960s; today the scene is dominated by the 270ft high Lowndes Tower.

North End buzzes with life, and everywhere we look notices advertising goods and services of one sort or another catch the eye, from Dr Scholls foot comfort service to superior ready to wear clothing - the kind of sign we never see today. Bespoke tailoring was far more common in the 1930s and 40s than it is now, when ready to wear clothing is taken for granted.

Those were the days, too, when stores employed delivery boys to convey the goods you had ordered right to your door - by way of a bicycle equipped with a large basket. What is the young man on the right carrying in his? It looks like half a dozen live chickens, though we can write that idea off as a 'probably not'! Fascinating, too, is the novel form of delivery vehicle

A glance at the 1930s

WHAT'S ON?

In this heyday of the cinema, horrified audiences were left gasping at the sight of Fay Wray in the clutches of the giant ape in the film 'King Kong', released in 1933. Very different but just as gripping was the gutsy 1939 American Civil War romance 'Gone with the Wind'. Gable's parting words, 'Frankly, my dear, I don't give a damn' went down in history.

GETTING AROUND

At the beginning of the decade many believed that the airship was the transport of the future. The R101 airship, however, loaded with thousands of cubic metres of hydrogen, crashed in France on its maiden flight in 1930. Forty-eight passengers and crew lost their lives. In 1937 the Hindenburg burst into flames - the entire disaster caught on camera and described by a distraught reporter. The days of the airship were numbered.

SPORTING CHANCE

The black American Jesse Owens won a brilliant four world records in the 1936 Olympic Games in Berlin, thumbing the nose to Adolf Hitler's dreams of Aryan superiority. In a petty display Hitler walked out of the stadium and 'took his bat home'; later he refused to have his photograph taken with the victorious Owens.

in use on the far right, where an innovative trader is utilising an old pram to get his trays of loaves (or perhaps cabbages?) from A to B.

On the left, a young girl steps warily into the road on to the pedestrian crossing; it is interesting to note that although Belisha beacons are in place at the crossing, zebra lines have not yet been introduced.

Above: *This photograph dates from the 1940s, possibly from World War II, and one of the first things we notice about the scene is the conspicuous lack of cars in North End. Older readers who can count photography among their hobbies will remember the chemists Durbin & McBryde, where you could buy a lot more than patent medicines. Everything connected with cameras, film and developing could be purchased from their shop, which was sadly missed when it disappeared from the scene. Marks & Spencer, of course, have added their extension since this picture was taken, and they remain a firm favourite with many. M & S has suffered from an unfortunate 'fuddy-duddy' image in recent years, but the quality of its clothing and the excellence of its food department has never been in doubt. It remains the favourite store with thousands of shoppers, especially for good quality under and outer wear and food. Marks and Spencer began life in Britain in the early years of the 20th century when Marks' Penny Bazaar opened up in the market in Leeds, West Yorkshire.*

Right: *A busy Saturday is caught on camera as shoppers bearing bags and baskets make their leisurely way along High Street, which looked very different back in 1953, the year of the photograph. Looking northwards towards the George Street and Crown Hill cross roads, readers will immediately spot the cone-shaped tower that once topped the Burtons and Milletts building. Perhaps a few of our more mature readers will remember the building in the 1930s when it was The Crown - one of Croydon's oldest hostelries. The Crown was offering rooms and stabling facilities as long ago as the 14th century, and naturally enough Crown Hill owes its name to the old inn. For many years the name was used informally until at last officialdom bowed to the inevitable and gave Crown Hill its official blessing. The Crown closed around 1940, and menswear took over until redevelopment of the town centre gave us Barclays Bank. Milletts still have a presence in the town on the corner of High Street and Surrey Street.*

Croydon Local Studies Library

Left: Any scene that includes the Whitgift Almshouses is a familiar one to every Croydonian, and in fact this part of George Street has changed very little since the photograph was taken in 1958, though the church and Thrift's clock tower in the distance have now disappeared from the scene. Even the Westminster Bank is today still the NatWest - a rare circumstance in these days of change, where even the names above the shops seem to vary year by year. George Street was a major shopping area back in Victorian times. It owed its name to the George Inn, which once stood opposite the Almshouses. A rather gruesome tale, which may or may not be true, is linked with the old inn. After the unaccountable disappearance of a number of visitors staying at The George, suspicion settled on the landlady (afterwards dubbed 'Old Mother Hotwater') who is reputed to have killed them and cooked their dismembered bodies in her kitchen. Shades of Sweeney Todd....

Above: How many of our readers remember sampling their very first drink in The Railway Hotel? Directly opposite East Croydon Station, The Railway Hotel opened its doors in 1841 in response to needs generated by the station, which had begun operating that same year on the London and Brighton Railway. The Railway was a favourite watering hole for more than a few, though younger readers might have trouble even identifying this as George Street. The coming years were to see the removal of buildings on both sides of the road; Suttons, whose outer wall here informs passers by that Omo washing powder added brightness and that Senior Service were the best cigarette, was to be replaced by Essex House, a large modern office block that in turn was itself demolished. Exciting new developments in the late 1990s gave Croydon the new Tramlink, with George Street forming part of the new route. Trams were last seen in our streets in 1951, and the ambitious new tramway system was designed to take the town forward into the new millennium with a marvellous fanfare, if not of trumpets, at least of horns and bells!

A glance at the 1930s

HOT OFF THE PRESS
The years of the 1930s saw Adolf Hitler's sickening anti-Jewish campaign echoed in the streets of Britain. On 19th October 1936 Oswald Mosley's 7,000-strong British Union of Fascists clashed head on with thousands of Jews and Communists in London, resulting in 80 people being injured in the ensuing battle. Mosley and his 'blackshirts' later rampaged through the streets beating up Jews and smashing the windows of their businesses.

THE WORLD AT LARGE
In India, Gandhi's peaceful protests against British rule were gathering momentum. The Salt Laws were a great bone of contention: forced to buy salt from the British government, thousands of protestors marched to the salt works, intending to take it over in the name of the Indian people. Policemen and guards attacked the marchers, but not one of them fought back. Gandhi, who earned for himself the name 'Mahatma' - Great Soul - was assassinated in 1948.

ROYAL WATCH
The talking point of the early 1930s was the affair of the Prince of Wales, who later became King Edward VIII, and American divorcee Wallis Simpson. Faced with a choice, Edward gave up his throne for 'the woman I love' and spent the remainder of his life in exile. Many supported him, though they might not have been as keen to do so if they had been aware of his Nazi sympathies, kept strictly under wraps at the time.

How many readers remember the Black and White Milk Bar in North End? Across the length and breadth of the country, Milk Bars had become a common sight in virtually every high street, and Croydon was no exception. An ideal place to pop in for a glass of milk, a quick cup of tea or coffee, and a snack, these pleasant and cosy establishments remained popular until the late 50s, when they began to give way to

the 'coffee bar', whose very name sounded so much more sophisticated than the label 'milk bar', which began to be regarded as countrified and 'backwoodsy'. The 1950s were the heyday of home dressmaking, and the sewing machine came into its own. The boring 'make do and mend' era of the 1940s was over and Allders on the left of the photograph were only one of many stores which sold gaily patterned dress fabrics and curtaining by the yard. Simplicity, Style and Maudella were the favourite paper patterns to buy, and many were the dresses, skirts, blouses and lounge curtains with matching cushion covers created on the kitchen table during those busy evenings and weekends.

Below: Another busy shopping day in Croydon town centre, and large crowds of punters appear to be heading for home with their purchases. At least one boy or girl is bound to be happy when Dad gets home; note the man walking in the roadway pushing a small child's tricycle - a birthday present, perhaps, for his son or daughter? The scene is dominated by the Whitgift Almshouses, still in use today by elderly residents. The building dates from 1596, when Archbishop John Whitgift constructed it for the use of the poor. A number of applications have been made down the years for the demolition of the historic building, which have long created a bottleneck in George Street. Fortunately the applications were all rejected and the almshouses were classified as Grade 1 listed buildings. A sharp eye might spot the initials 'IW' for John Whitgift (the letter J was not added to the English alphabet until the 17th century), picked out in brickwork on the gable nearest us in the photograph. Readers will also notice the newer brickwork which formed part of the repairs made to the building after bomb damage in World War II.

Right: Doesn't it seems strange to see traffic in North End? The Hillman Minx, once the pride and joy of thousands of motorists, takes centre stage. Today, shoppers have no need to look both ways before crossing the road and are able to browse in pleasant, tree-lined surroundings in traffic-free safety. Parents with prams and young children are especially grateful for the safety of the pedestrian precinct.
North End has long been noted for its shopping facilities, and includes the big names such as Allders, Littlewoods and Debenhams and, of course, the Whitgift Centre. Horne Brothers tailors can be seen on the right; gentlemen's outfitting has long been a trade to attract many rivals: Greenwoods, Hepworths, Hope Brothers, Moss Bros and Austin Reed, with Hector Powe at the top end of the market, and for the ordinary man in the street Alkit, who specialised in cheaper clothing. The rival firm Hepworths eventually managed to acquire the services of the Queen's own designer.

Bottom: Captured for posterity, a white Triumph Herald convertible turns into High Street, where most of the names above the shop fronts differed from those of today. The picture dates from 1963, and in the background we can catch a glimpse of Grants department store which unfortunately did not survive past the early 1980s. Milletts, however, still occupies the same position on the corner of Surrey Street. Milletts has long been a name to be reckoned with in the realm of workwear, and branches of the popular store can be seen across the UK. Duffle coats, trousers, jackets, shirts, boots, you name it - if it was workwear - and you could almost certainly buy it at Milletts. Stuffed to bursting point with an immense range of goods, this store was the obvious port of call for any man who needed either working gear or casual clothes. The Davis Theatre had already disappeared from High Street when this view was snapped, though Cullens and the Brighter Homes store occupied part of the theatre building.

Right: Long hair, mini skirts, and tights that allowed hemlines to rise so high, were badges of the 1960s, and this scene snapped in North End in 1967 captures the essence of the decade. The young woman towards the right of the picture was obviously a dedicated follower of fashion; at the time the country was in the grip of flower power, girls had burnt their bras (emotionally if not actually), psychedelic purples, shocking pinks and brash yellows were in and the tight perms and flowing skirts of the previous decade were most definitely out.

This was the heyday of boutiques, where the younger generation congregated to shop for their short dresses with flowing sleeves, and the ankle-strap shoes and knee length boots that had ousted the pointed toes of a few years earlier. A short time on, the vagaries of fashion would turn the spotlight on hot pants and fun fur. Is the warmly-dressed gentleman walking alongside the girl her father? In the 1960s men's fashions moved far more slowly than did women's, and the knee-length 'car coat' was to remain popular wear for many years.

At leisure

The John Gent Collection

'Secret of the Chateau' and 'The Green Pack' were being screened at the Scala when this scene was captured for posterity, though we are left guessing about who were the stars of these little known films. By the 1930s the Scala had become part of Allders, with a side door that connected with the arcade, though when it was constructed in 1914 it actually adjoined the department store. World War I was in progress at the time, and the cinema's staff were taken from those who were exempt from military service. Those were the days when the price of admission guaranteed you a full programme that included a 'B' movie, the latest news, a cartoon, trailers of forthcoming attractions and the 'big picture'. Over the years the 880-seat Scala went into decline and a sudden decision was made to close the cinema in March 1952. The last programme included 'Monte Cristo's Revenge' and 'The Lady from Tangier'.

Think of the Davis Theatre, and the memories come flooding back. Some of our readers might even remember seeing 'Rally Round the Flag, Boys' and 'The Lavender Hill Mob', being screened at the time of the photograph, which was taken not long before the cinema closed. 'Rally Round the Flag, Boys' was a sex comedy starring Paul Newman and Joanne Woodward, though reviewers decided that it raised very few laughs. In a different class altogether was 'The Lavender Hill Mob', a film hailed as one of the best comedies ever produced in Britain. The Davis Theatre was opened in December 1928 as a cinema, though it was well equipped to produce live theatre and even opera and ballet. When it was built, the elegant Davis Theatre, with more than 3,700 seats, was the second largest cinema in Britain. Its ballroom and cafe, royal circle with luxurious armchair seats, and its magnificent four-manual organ all added to the cinema's impressive facilities. It even had a lift to carry patrons to the back of the stalls - an unusual feature in cinemas and theatres. Television took off in a big way during the 1950s, sadly spelling the end for many local cinemas. Many fought valiantly on as bingo clubs and snooker halls, but the Davis sadly closed in May 1959 and was later demolished.

The John Gent Collection

The John Gent Collection

Croydon Local Studies Library

siasts. In those days before motorised transport, many customers travelled by horse-drawn vehicles, and the Derby Arms provided excellent stabling facilities for their visitors. The pub was renamed in 1992 as The Paddock.

Top: The Greyhound Restaurant was an impressive establishment when this photograph was taken in the 1930s, and it was to remain a favourite eating house with many locals until it closed in 1959. Another of Croydon's historic hostelries, The Greyhound had extensive premises and excellent stabling facilities. In 1926 the old inn underwent major alterations, and during the work builders uncovered (and sadly damaged) an inscription which dated from Tudor times. It was a poignant quotation from the Bible (Psalm 103:15), reminding us of the splendour - and the brevity - of life: 'As for man, his days are like grass; as a flower of the field, so he flourishes.' The hand that wrote the inscription - along with those who read the words when the work was newly completed - turned to dust more than 400 years ago.

In November 1959 this splendid building had also disappeared, and by the early 1960s its modern successor was offering customers a lunch time a la carte service in Park Lane.

Above: This well-assorted though equally fascinating selection of vehicles was snapped in Pitlake in August 1961, and one thing we immediately spot is the lack of double yellow lines along the edge of the road. In those long ago days before the advent of multi-storey car parks and expensive parking, motorists could usually find a convenient spot to leave their car outside the office or near the shops. Will the drivers of these cars fill up with BP at the Handcroft Services before leaving for home? The Derby Arms dominates the background of this nostalgic scene; the pub was built in 1832 and became well known as a centre for hunting enthu-

Below: A prominent sign above the canopy of the Grand Theatre tells us that seats for their twice nightly variety shows have 'Popular Prices'; wouldn't it be fascinating to know what those prices were? The photograph was taken in the 1930s, the heyday of the variety show, and an evening's entertainment programme might include a couple of singers, a comic duo, acrobats and musicians - some famous, others further down the bill, not so much so - and the public would go home satisfied at the end of the evening having enjoyed a varied and most enjoyable night out. Many would head for the nearest tram stop, while the more affluent among the audience would collect their cars from the theatre's own car park - quite an innovation back in the 1930s, when only the better-off could afford to run their own vehicle. The Grand closed in 1959 after charming audiences for a total of 63 years, and was sadly demolished. Were any of our readers present at the last show?

The 1930s were the heyday of the variety show

Events & occasions

Croydon Local Studies Library

Both pictures: In the 1920s and 30s the Great War was still fresh in the minds of Croydonians, many of whom had lost more than one family member on the field of battle. Not too many years previously in a railway carriage in France, Germany had surrendered to the Allies, the Kaiser had abdicated and fled into exile in Holland, and the four-year war had officially ended at the 11th hour of the 11th day of the 11th month. Every year thereafter, a two-minutes' silence was observed at 11am on November 11th out of respect for those whose lives were prematurely ended by the conflict; an appalling total of 8.5 million people were killed in the Great War. The annual two-minutes' silence became a tradition, and across the UK everyday life came to a standstill as people stood respectfully in the street and traffic

came to a halt. Vast crowds gathered in Katharine Street on Armistice Day in 1926 *(below)*; at the time, the dates 1914 to 1918 stood alone on the war memorial (unveiled five years earlier on 22nd October 1921), with the words 'A tribute to the men and women of Croydon who died and suffered'. We now know that the Great War did not turn out to be 'the war that ended all wars'; the future held yet more suffering and loss for the people of Croydon, and the dates 1939 to 1945 were later added to the cenotaph with the legend 'And in memory of those who lost their lives in wars and conflicts since.'

Armistice Day, 1930, saw yet another gathering, and members of the British Legion, proudly wearing an impressive array of medals, prepare to lay the customary wreath of poppies at the war memorial *(above)*.

Croydon Local Studies Library

It was June 1933; Croydon had been a Borough for 50 years, and when the President of Croydon Chamber of Commerce suggested decorations the town seized on the concept and the end product far surpassed his original modest idea. An invitation was sent to Prince George (the fourth son of King George V), asking him to lay the foundation stone of the General Hospital's new wing during the Incorporation celebrations, neatly killing two birds with one stone, as it were.

Flags of all nations were strung across the streets, and shops, businesses and private houses added their own decorations to the official ones. The large stores such as Kennards and Allders not only decorated their premises with flags and bunting, but they also hung banners across the street, welcoming Prince George to the town. The entire town centre was awash with colour. It was the Town Hall Gardens, however, that were the real pièce de resistance; they had become the province of Croydon's Electricity Department, and they turned the gardens into a fairyland that back in 1933 would have been a rare sight. An electric fountain threw jets of water 15ft into the air, with coloured lights playing on the water, while every flower bed was outlined with streamers of fairy lights and trees were festooned with lanterns. What a sight that must have been!

Croydon Local Studies Library

Above: The streets of Croydon were a riot of red, white and blue when the charming and popular Prince of Wales, with Princess Alexandra, visited the town to declare the new Town Hall officially open. The date was 19th May 1896, and it was a proud day for the people of Croydon, who had watched the construction of the beautiful building of red brick and Portland stone. The first brick had been laid four years earlier on 9th March 1892 by Mrs Frederick Edridge, the Mayoress. This was Croydon's third Town Hall, and for the time was very innovative, being lit by electricity instead of the more usual gas lighting, and with a telephone system connecting its offices. Croydon turned out in full force to welcome the royal couple, and the celebrations continued until late into the evening, with illuminations and a fireworks display. Prince Edward, the eldest son of Queen Victoria and Prince Albert, was 59 when he at last became King Edward VII. Having earned Queen Victoria's disapproval, he was denied any access to state papers and was ill-prepared for his role as King. His reign was a short one - he died on 6th May 1910.

When King George V died in 1936, he was genuinely mourned by the whole nation. The people of Croydon turned out in full force, and gathered in Katharine Street to honour the memory of a good man and a great King. George Duke of York came to the throne in 1910. The model of the ideal Englishman, King George made himself immensely popular with his subjects without really trying. He was tolerant of people whose opinions differed from his own - but not afraid to speak his mind when the occasion called for straight talking. Dignified, fair, conscientious and modest, he once remarked on the warmth with which people

Croydon Local Studies Library

greeted him during his Silver Jubilee celebrations, 'I am beginning to think they like me for myself.' George V was the first monarch to broadcast a Christmas Day message over the radio; the Christmas Broadcast became the established tradition that we still enjoy today. King George's widow, Queen Mary, lived on until 1953.

A glance at the 1930s

MELODY MAKERS
Throughout the 1930s a young American trombonist called Glenn Miller was making his mark in the world of music. By 1939 the Glenn Miller sound was a clear leader in the field; his clean-cut, meticulously executed arrangements of numbers such as 'A String of Pearls' and 'Moonlight Serenade' brought him fame across the world as a big-band leader. During a flight to England from Paris in 1944 Miller's plane disappeared; no wreckage was ever found.

HOT OFF THE PRESS
The years of the 1930s saw Adolf Hitler's sickening anti-Jewish campaign echoed in the streets of Britain. On 19th October 1936 Oswald Mosley's 7,000-strong British Union of Fascists clashed head on with thousands of Jews and Communists in London, resulting in 80 people being injured in the ensuing battle. Mosley and his 'blackshirts' later rampaged through the streets beating up Jews and smashing the windows of their businesses.

SCIENCE AND DISCOVERY
By observing the heavens, astronomers had long believed that there in the constellation of Gemini lay a new planet, so far undiscovered. They began to search for the elusive planet, and a special astronomical camera was built for the purpose. The planet Pluto was discovered by amateur astronomer Clyde Tombaugh in 1930, less than a year later.

Shopping - at the heart of Croydon for over 30 years

Say 'Whitgift' to anyone in Croydon today, and the first thing that springs to mind is 'shopping'. This is hardly surprising; The Whitgift Shopping Centre, built during the late 60s and officially opened in 1970, brought Croydon the distinction of being home to the largest Shopping Centre of its kind anywhere in Europe, and furthermore it has remained one of the country's most successful and well-established retail centres ever since. In recent years The Whitgift's refurbishment has given an extra boost to this shoppers' paradise at the heart of Croydon. With more than 150 stores and restaurants laid out in stylish and elegant surroundings, The Whitgift has created a retail environment second to none, which will provide millions of people with their ultimate shopping experience in the year 2000 - the year in which The Whitgift celebrates its 30th anniversary.

For today's younger generations, trying to imagine Croydon without The Whitgift must be very difficult - rather like trying to picture life before the Internet was invented. However, older readers will still remember a time prior to 1965 when the Trinity School of John Whitgift stood in North End. Readers with even longer memories may recall, too, that up until 1931 North End was the home of Whitgift Grammar School, which is now known simply as Whitgift School and will soon be celebrating its 400th anniversary at its new site at Haling Park. In fact, a significant proportion of our readers will have been to school on the place where now we all go to do our shopping.

The Whitgift connection with education in Croydon can be traced back to the 16th century, when plans for a Hospital (now known as the Almshouses) and School were formulated by John Whitgift, Archbishop of Canterbury. John Whitgift was one of the best-known and most highly-respected figures of his day. The name 'Whitgift' signifies 'white gift', and is an entirely fitting name for a man who gave so much of lasting value to Croydon before his death in 1604; indeed, looking round our town today, it is difficult to overestimate the impact which his legacy has had on the our lives over the centuries. Both the Whitgift School at Haling Park and the Trinity School of John Whitgift at Shirley Park can trace their origins back to the School which he established alongside the Hospital in 1600. Each of these schools in turn was accom-

Above left: *John Whitgift, Archbishop of Canterbury, who first began to plan a school for Croydon in 1595.*
Below: *The entrance to Trinity School in the early 1960s.*

world war that the Croydon of the future began to take shape.

By this time Croydon's sights were firmly set on change. Since the natural focus of the town was the area around Wellesley Road, George Street and North End, it was this part which was destined to become, in one way or another, the business and commercial centre of the town; so it was a fortunate co-incidence that the Whitgift's former school site on North End should become available for development at just the right time. From 1947 onwards a succession of Town Planning schemes had been produced by Croydon Corporation, each of which had become the subject of lengthy debate. There were many factors to be taken into consideration and balanced one against the other. There were local factors such as Croydon's increasing population, its growing importance as a commercial and retail centre and its potential for further expansion; there were regional factors such as its status as one of the largest of the London boroughs, and its position at the centre of an increasingly complex network of road and rail systems which had led to it becoming in effect an extension to the City and West End of London; and there were general factors such as the rise in popularity of the motor car, the greater affluence of society and its new focus on youth fashions and consumer goods in general.

While Croydon Corporation was discussing these and other matters and seeking to establish an overall development strategy which would please all sectors of the community, in the mid 60s the Whitgift Foundation, in partnership with Ravenseft Properties Limited, began to form plans for a complementary project - the development of a self-contained 12-acre commercial unit which was to occupy the prime position in the heart of the town.

modated at the North End site at a later stage in their history. Whitgift School occupied the site between 1871 and 1931. Trinity School moved there in 1931, but by the early 60s it had outgrown the premises and was planning to move to the outskirts of Croydon. Their move signalled the beginning of a new and exciting era in the history of the North End site, which had been part of the Whitgift Estate for so long.

By the time Trinity School vacated North End in the mid-60s this spot had been the site of a school for not far short of a century, and Croydon had changed enormously in that time. Incredible as it seems today, part of the site used to be a large field which stretched across to Wellesley Road; before becoming the School sports field in 1871, this piece of open land had for many years been used by the townsfolk for cricket matches and archery contests. The early 20th century had brought the recognition that the future development of the town should be planned to reflect the growth in the population of Croydon and the town's increasing commercial activity. However, it was not until the end of the second

Top: *An aerial view of Trinity School in 1961.*
Above left: *An early visit by the Queen to the Almshouses in 1983.* **Right:** *The demolition of the school to make way for The Whitgift Shopping Centre.*

This superior development was to consist of a modern pedestrian shopping area together with offices designed to the provide the very highest standards of accommodation.

The concept of the shopping centre was still new to us in Britain at this time, and this was to be the largest traffic-free shop and office precincts in the country. In view of its pioneering nature a tremendous amount of research was carried out, including public consultations and discussions with the large retailers, before construction began in 1965, and a great number of ingenious features were incorporated into the scheme. For instance, its design took advantage of the natural slope of the ground, so that shoppers approaching on foot from Wellesley Road could walk directly into the upper level of the two-level, traffic-free shopping area, while the entrances from North End led onto the lower shopping level. Altogether five pedestrian entrances were planned: there were two on North End - the main entrance being where the main entrance to the School used to be, with another being Chapel Walk - and two on Wellesley Road, with a further entrance in Poplar Walk, while the Centre could also be reached via Allders Arcade. For shoppers coming into Croydon by car, ample parking was provided in the Wellesley Road multi-storey car park, with easy walk-through access into the shopping malls, while the proximity of East Croydon and West Croydon stations made it just as easy to travel in by train.

The development itself was on three storeys, with the upper two levels forming the retail floors while the basement provided access for vehicles along a one-kilometre network of service roads, with a one-way system which made delivering goods to any of the retail units a simple business. In this way shoppers were able to enjoy the advantages of a pedestrian-only shopping environment, without the slightest inconvenience being passed on to the stores. Most stores on the lower shopping level were designed to have direct access into their storerooms from the basement, while goods lifts were provided for the use of those on the upper level. The close integration of office accommodation and retail units within the development was in itself another very positive feature, bringing obvious advantages both for retailers and office workers.

Below: *The construction of the 21 storey Rothschild House.*
Bottom: *The construction of the new shopping centre.*

two options, as it housed a pub upstairs and a restaurant downstairs. Another important bene-fit of this enclosed shopping environment which many shoppers were barely even aware of was the constant surveillance by professional security guards, whose presence acted as an effective deterrent to criminals and trouble-makers alike and made the Shopping Centre an ideal place for families.

By 1969 the major part of this revolutionary addition to Croydon's town centre was complete, with only the finishing touches to be added. The long-awaited official opening ceremony was performed in October 1970 by the Duchess of Kent; more than 3,000 shoppers and office

Top: An aerial view of The Whitgift site shortly after completion of construction in 1969.
Above left: North End entrance in January 1966 after Trinity School was demolished.
Below: Boots - the first store to open at the centre in 1968.

Once construction was under way, everybody who came to Croydon with any regularity began to follow the growth process of the new Shopping Centre with avid interest. The very first shop to open was Boots, on 17th October 1968, and from then on there was something new to discover, week by week: more new shops, newly-completed decorative features and another place to get a cup of coffee. The Whitgift became part of people's regular shopping routine, and as the number and variety of stores inside the shopping centre grew, shop-pers found that they could get everything they needed there - food, clothes, toys, furniture - you name it! There was no longer any need for them to pick their way through the traffic on the main streets; and what was more, lengthy family shopping expeditions could be punctuated by tasty snacks at the various refreshment establishments scattered around the Shopping Centre, or a spot of purely liquid refreshment to keep one's strength up, or even a main meal - The Merchants Arms Pub (later The Forum) could cater for either of the last

workers crowded into the shopping centre for the occasion, and no doubt they were all proud to count themselves customers of The Whitgift Shopping Centre and members of the Croydon community when they read the Duchess's comments as reported in the Press, afterwards: 'I am completely fascinated,' she had said. 'Why doesn't every town in the country have something like this?'

Royalty is not easily impressed; but The Whitgift, with its sales area of 35,000 square feet, was not only one of the largest shopping precincts in the south of England, but also one of the most attractive. With such a tremendous range of goods to be found there, it became a talking-point among all those who knew Croydon: 'Have you seen what they've got in The Whitgift?' 'I wonder where I can get a present for my mum . . . I know, I'll try The Whitgift!' 'Are you going into Croydon on Saturday? Let's meet in the Whitgift at ten o'clock!' Its fame spread rapidly by word of mouth, and so, having recorded an immediate and resounding success

Above: The Forum Pub in 1984. Right: The Mall looking towards Sainsbury's Square in 1973.
Below: The Wellesley Road entrance in the early 1970s.

among retailers and local shoppers alike, the new Shopping Centre was soon attracting visitors from all over the south-east of England. Many of these paid an initial visit prompted by curiosity, just to see what everyone was talking about - and then returned time after time when they discovered that shopping in Croydon had taken on an entirely new aspect. A wander along The Whitgift's pleasant shopping malls brought the shopper to most of the town's most popular shops, one after the other - Allders, established in Croydon as a small shop more than a century ago and now the third largest department store in the country, was located there from the outset, alongside a growing number of old favourites and exciting newcomers. Virtually every consumer need was catered for by the 220 or so retail units, and in the pleasant environment created by the planners, shopping had become a pleasure instead of a chore.

selection of shops and setting new standards of shopping comfort.

The tremendous impact of the Shopping Centre arose out of its success in predicting and meeting the needs and wishes of the shopper, and it remained keenly alert to any new ways in which it could improve the services it offered to its customers. In 1985 it responded to the move towards providing consumers with a wider choice in the times at which they could do their shopping by introducing late night opening. Stores remained open until nine o'clock in the evening every Thursday, and Tuesdays as well during late November and December. Meanwhile it continued to look at new ideas aimed at improving the retail environment, and by 1986 it had identified a wide enough range of potential improvements to justify a major refurbishment and modernisation programme.

During the 30 years or so since the opening of the new Shopping Centre, generations of shoppers have grown up safe in the knowledge that The Whitgift is the best place to shop. An inevitable result of this process of evolution is that features which were perceived by one generation as representing the ultimate in convenience and luxury were merely taken for granted by the next. So, as we approach The Whitgift's 30th anniversary, it is perhaps fitting that we should stop for a moment and picture ourselves back in 1970, and try to remember - or imagine, in the case of those readers who are too young to remember - what a revelation it must have been, to have a brand-new kind of Shopping Centre opening in our town, easily accessible by public transport or by car, bringing together an excellent

Above left: The Mall at Christmas in the early 1970s.
Above right: North End entrance as it was in the 1970s.
Below: Allders Square - 1974.

tions; the mall cafe draws many thirsty shoppers to the former, while the latter, with its two water features ornamented with bamboo, provides an attractive setting for fashion shows and other organised entertainment. In addition to these two squares, new arcades were built and 25 new retail units were constructed to give the shopper even more choice. Phase Two also included the installation of the two lifts and the escalator in Whitgift Square and the scenic lift and escalator in Allders Square, the installation of roofing over a large part of the remainder of the shopping centre, and improved public conveniences including facilities for the disabled and a parent and baby room.

The first phase commenced in November 1986, and involved the demolition and redevelopment of the former North End Odeon cinema, the erection of new roofing over the central malls between Marks & Spencer and H Samuel, the laying of Terrazzo flooring, the installation of new escalators and new lighting, and updating the internal decor. Improvements continued for almost three years, and the total cost of this phase was in the region of £10 million; one particularly innovative and impressive feature is the climatically-controlled skylights in the glass roof, which open automatically on hot days and let in fresh air.

Even more excitement was generated by the second phase of the programme, which resulted in a considerable increase in the overall area of The Whitgift through the demolition in April 1993 of the Forum Pub and surrounding buildings. Both the Allders Square and Whitgift Square were re-created during this phase, and they have both become great attrac-

Above: *East Arcade during refurbishment in early 1994. In this picture one half of the roof has already been constructed.* **Below:** *Wellesley Road entrance as it is today.* **Bottom:** *The Mall as it is today.*

Once again the planners got it exactly right. A glance at the photographs which appear on these pages will show what a difference the new roof, the escalators, the lighting, the flooring and the new decor have made. A total of nearly 160 shop units - including the giant stores of Allders, Marks & Spencer and Woolworths - now share an immense shopping area of approximately 1.2 million square feet, making The Whitgift one of the country's top five shopping complexes. The addition of the third-floor restaurant is another definite bonus for many visitors, of whom some 600,000 a week, or 30 million a year, pass through the entrances of The Whitgift.

And wherever they come from, today's shoppers find it easier than ever to get to The Whitgift; public transport and road links have improved tremendously in the last 30 years and further improvements are imminent. With the M23/M25 interchange only nine miles away and Central London less than a quarter of an hour away by train, those wishing to travel in an east-west direction - notoriously difficult in the past - will soon benefit from the new Croydon Tramlink service which will be open before the end of 1999 to connect with Beckenham and Wimbledon. Meanwhile, with 9,500 convenient car parking spaces available drivers can rely on finding a parking space; so the many people who use The Whitgift as a rendez-vous point can be sure of arriving on time, and of enjoying a happy and fruitful day's shopping. Whatever their personal circumstances - whether they live or work nearby and pop into The Whitgift several times a week, or whether they can only get into Croydon every now and again - every visit to the newly-refurbished Whitgift Shopping Centre is a special occasion.

So, once again, The Whitgift has been successful in exceeding expectations and providing that extra touch of luxury which never fails to delight; and as The Whitgift approaches its 30th anniversary, it is still a talking-point in Croydon and the south east, and a favourite and indispensable part of many people's lives.

Left: *North End entrance today.*
Top: *Whitgift Square as it is today.*
Below: *Tramlink opening in November 1999. The tram stops outside the Wellesley Road entrance to The Whitgift Shopping Centre.*

Wartime

Both pictures: *In 1938 Adolf Hitler had signed the Munich Agreement and Britain's Prime Minister, Neville Chamberlain, made the mistake of trusting him. Many, however, had no confidence in Hitler and did not believe Chamberlain's assurance of 'peace in our time'; they continued to prepare for a war that they still saw as inevitable. On 6th May 1939 huge crowds turned out to line the streets of Croydon to watch a procession that was an incredible two miles long. Organised by the Home Defence, the aim of the event was to pull in hundreds of people who were willing to volunteer to defend the country should war break out. Everyone loves a parade, especially if there is a rousing band to keep the spectators' feet tapping and the marchers in step, and this lengthy parade had many bands. The Brigade of Guards led the way, with pipers and drummers in swinging kilts, and every service and organisation from St John Ambulance Brigade to detachments of the Coldstream and Grenadier Guards processed behind, with bands placed at intervals between the marchers. Speeches calling for Croydonians to do their patriotic duty were made along the route, and in Katharine Street the Mayor and Mayoress added their own appeal. Britain declared war on Germany four months later on 3rd September.*

The camera captures a sad moment as troops say goodbye to their wives and families, and a forlorn little boy snuggles close to Daddy for the last time before he goes off to war. For some who waved their loved ones off from Croydon Barracks in Mitcham Road that day it would be the final goodbye, and this possibility had to have been uppermost in all of their minds. 'Take care of yourself, Darling,' would have been often repeated at the scene - though these were no more than empty words to men who perhaps had no idea where they were bound for and who had no control over where an enemy shell or bomb might land. Wartime was possibly the worst time to forge relationships and

A glance at the 1940s

MELODY MAKERS
The songs of radio personalities such as Bing Crosby and Vera Lynn were whistled, sung and hummed everywhere during the 1940s. The 'forces' sweetheart' brought hope to war-torn Britain with 'When the Lights go on Again', while the popular crooner's 'White Christmas' is still played around Christmas time even today. Who can forget songs like 'People Will Say we're in Love', and 'Riders in the Sky'?

INVENTION AND TECHNOLOGY
Inspired by quick-drying printers' ink, in 1945 Hungarian journalist Laszlo Biro developed a ballpoint pen which released viscous ink from its own reservoir as the writer moved the pen across the page. An American inventor was working on a similar idea at the same time, but it was Biro's name that stuck. A few years later Baron Bich developed a low cost version of the pen, and the 'Bic' ballpoint went on sale in France in 1953.

SCIENCE AND DISCOVERY
In 1943 Ukrainian-born biochemist Selman Abraham Waksman made a significant discovery. While studying organisms found in soil he discovered an antibiotic (a name Waksman himself coined) which was later found to be the very first effective treatment for tuberculosis. A major killer for thousands of years, even the writings of the ancient Egyptians contain stories of people suffering from tuberculosis. Waksman's development of streptomycin brought him the 1952 Nobel Prize for Medicine.

marry, yet incredibly more couples than ever decided to tie the knot in the first months of the war. Half a million weddings took place in 1940 as men were called up to join the military, though the usual bridal trappings were virtually unobtainable. Honeymoons, taken for granted today, were often non-existent as the groom kissed his bride and went straight back to war.

Croydon Local Studies Library

Above: During the second world war Air Raid Prevention staff needed the expertise to deal with unfamiliar situations, including the horrendous injuries suffered by bomb victims. First aid was high on the list of skills to be acquired, and this exercise was intended to help them to decide what immediate treatment was necessary to save lives. A selection of 'victims' with varying symptoms lie along the pavement, and diagnosis, we see, has already been done for the benefit of the hard-pressed ARP workers. What would they do for the unconscious man in the foreground with an abdominal wound, we wonder? Would the man with head injuries receive the correct treatment for his concussion? And what about the poor guy whose right hand had been severed? Nasty one, this, if he was not to bleed to death. Number four in line, who has a broken clavicle, fractured ribs and concussion, is not taking his acting role very seriously and is looking rather sprightly for someone who is supposed to be deeply unconscious.... When it came to the realities of war, ARP wardens performed exceptional work in dealing with incendiaries, giving first aid to the injured, helping to rescue victims from their bombed-out properties, clearing away rubble, and a thousand and one other tasks.

Above right: This fascinating wartime photograph compares a Local Defence Volunteer of 1940 with his counterpart - by that time the 32nd Surrey Battalion Home Guard - in 1944. When war broke out in 1939, Sir Anthony Eden, the Secretary of State for War, made a radio appeal for men outside military age to volunteer for membership of the LDV to defend their country in the event of Nazi invasion. Teenagers of 17 and able-bodied

Croydon Local Studies Library

senior citizens all rushed to put their names down; many of the amateur soldiers had never before wielded so much as a broom handle in anger, but every one of them was prepared to do his or her bit for Britain. The member of LDV on the left has no uniform and no weapons; at first the new force had to improvise, and men had to rely on sticks, shotguns handed in by local people, and on sheer determination. In July 1940 the LDV was renamed the Home Guard, and weapons and uniforms gradually became available.

Mobile canteens, usually staffed by the Women's Voluntary Service and other volunteer agencies, became a familiar sight around Croydon's streets when the bombs began to fall during World War II. The canteen was obviously a cheering sight to these troops caught by the photographer in North End as they pause, mugs of tea in hand, for a well-earned break; one soldier has obviously enjoyed his cuppa so much that he is holding out hopefully for a second cup!

The volunteer services who staffed the mobile canteens did much marvellous work during the war, bringing hot drinks, food and comfort to people who had lost their homes or their cooking facilities in air raids, and giving a much needed lift to Civil Defence workers and the fire services at incident sites. A hot mug of tea was often just what they needed as they battled with coolness and courage hour after hour in unbelievable conditions to rescue people from their damaged homes.

By kind permission of the Croydon Advertiser Group

Croydon Local Studies Library

The late 1930s brought the fear of war to Britain. Many believed it would not happen at all, others thought that if it did it would be over very quickly. In spite of Chamberlain's attempts to appease Adolf Hitler preparations began to alert the citizens of Britain to the dangers of a conflict that many believed was inevitable. Able-bodied men and women were encouraged to join the military or sign up as Civil Defence workers. This exhibition and demonstration of war equipment is thought to have been part of the recruitment drive, and crowds of passers by have paused

to examine the air raid sirens, spotlights and communications being displayed. To the right of the photograph a number of people are being shown how to use gas masks. At the time, local air raid precautions organisations were established in every district and air raid wardens were appointed and trained. The Home Office prepared a booklet entitled 'The Protection of your Home against Air Raids' which was sent to every home in Britain. It encouraged every home and family to play an active part 'if this country were ever at war'.

Croydon Local Studies Library

Croydon Local Studies Library

Home Guard, Women's Auxiliaries and Civil Defence workers. All had played their own valuable part throughout the war, and now it was time to allow the smiles to break out on tired faces, let down the hair and party!

Six years of war had worn everyone down, and as soon as peace was declared Croydon went wild with joy. Bunting was strung from house to house across every street, patriotic flags flapped gaily in the breeze, and street parties, fireworks displays and bonfires were organised in every community around the town.

Both pages: Parades had become part and parcel of everyday life throughout World War II; they kept ordinary people in touch with the military and made them feel part of the war effort. This parade, however, was different. This time, the marchers had a lighter step, for victory was theirs and this was Croydon's Thanksgiving Parade. Every service and organisation formed part of the mile-long procession: following the band of the London Fire Service were representatives of the Royal Artillery, the Royal Electrical and Mechanical Engineers, the Scots Guards, the RAF, the

It was Britain's new Prime Minister, Clement Attlee, who brought the nation down from its euphoria with a resounding bump. He gave the country a serious warning that although Britain was once more at peace, there was no likelihood of prosperity for the country in the immediate future. Across the world countries were decimated by war, and there were worldwide food shortages. It would be several more years before people could stop using tinned dried eggs or shop for clothes without counting how many coupons they had.

This page:
Children loved the excitement of the rousing bands and the marching soldiers. A crowd has gathered in Katharine Street to watch this particular parade, and the camera has captured the 32nd Surrey Battalion

Croydon Local Studies Library

them, though weapons and uniforms did not become available for several months. A few months on, the Local Defence Volunteers was renamed the Home Guard. Television programmes such

Home Guard as they pass the cenotaph. The scene below is an uncommon one, as mounted detachments of the Home Guard were rare.

At the start of the second world war Sir Anthony Eden, Secretary of State for War, appealed in a radio broadcast for men between 17 and 65 to make up a new force, the Local Defence Volunteers, to guard vulnerable points from possible attack in the event of invasion by Germany. Within hours the first men were eagerly putting their names down.

They trained hard to meet the standards required of

as 'Dad's Army' have unfortunately associated the Home Guard with comedy, but the force, even if amateur, was very well organised and in fact they performed a huge amount of important work. The Guard posted sentries to watch for possible aircraft or parachute landings at likely spots such as disused aerodromes, golf courses on the outskirts of towns, local parks and racecourses. They manned anti-aircraft rocket guns, liaised with other units and with regular troops, set up communications and organised balloon barrages.

Croydon Local Studies Library

Croydon Local Studies Library

This page: When war in Europe ended in 1945, a lot of hard work lay ahead as people looked towards creating a better and peaceful future for themselves and their families. But before that there was time to reflect on the gains and losses of the long conflict, to give thanks to God that they had beaten the enemy and had survived - and to mourn the loss of so many in Croydon who didn't make it. On Tuesday 8th May 1945, a VE Day thanksgiving service was held outside the Town Hall in Katharine Street. It was a day of mixed feelings, and one which few among the huge crowd who gathered in the town centre to hear the Prime Minister's official announcement that the war in Europe was over will ever forget. The Mayor, Cllr George Lewin, led the service, which was followed by scenes of real jubilation as Croydonians took to the streets and danced for joy.

Though a number of people held back their celebrations until peace was gained in Japan, many were the parties, dances, bonfires and scenes of gaiety that heralded the declaration of victory in Europe - and many were the effigies of Hitler that were burnt on bonfires around Croydon! Vengeance, however sweet, was not theirs, however. Adolf Hitler had already departed this life to be judged by a higher authority; forsaking his dream of a thousand-year Reich, he and Eva Braun had committed suicide together just the week before, on 30th April. In the Pacific the war was to continue for a further four months; the Japanese surrendered on August 14th.

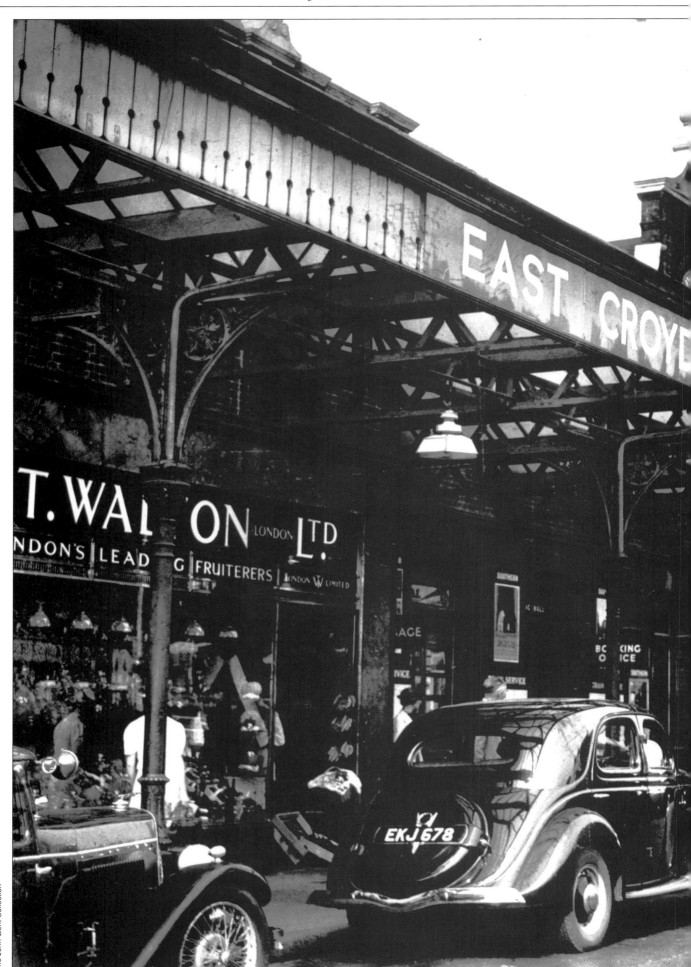

On the move

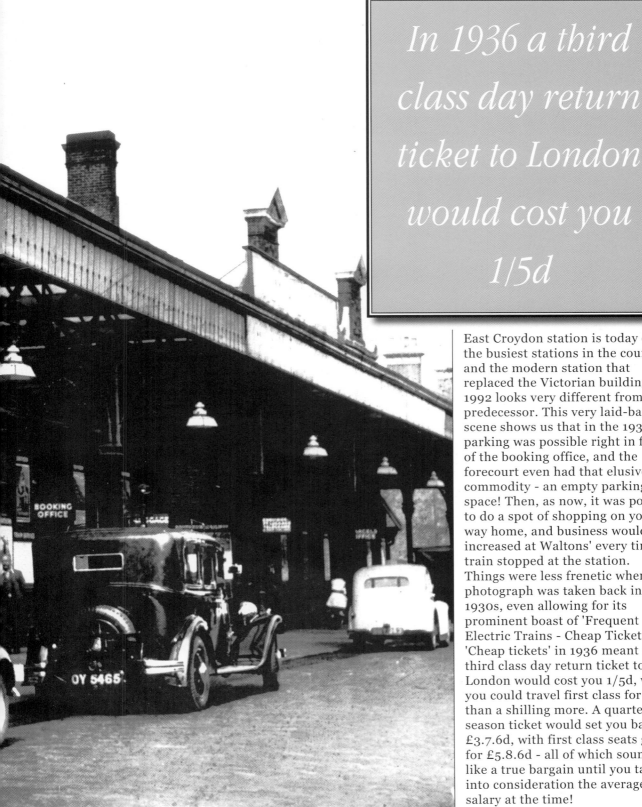

> In 1936 a third class day return ticket to London would cost you 1/5d

East Croydon station is today one of the busiest stations in the country, and the modern station that replaced the Victorian building in 1992 looks very different from its predecessor. This very laid-back scene shows us that in the 1930s parking was possible right in front of the booking office, and the forecourt even had that elusive commodity - an empty parking space! Then, as now, it was possible to do a spot of shopping on your way home, and business would have increased at Waltons' every time a train stopped at the station. Things were less frenetic when this photograph was taken back in the 1930s, even allowing for its prominent boast of 'Frequent Electric Trains - Cheap Tickets'. 'Cheap tickets' in 1936 meant that a third class day return ticket to London would cost you 1/5d, while you could travel first class for less than a shilling more. A quarterly season ticket would set you back £3.7.6d, with first class seats going for £5.8.6d - all of which sounds like a true bargain until you take into consideration the average salary at the time!

Croydon Local Studies Library

Both pages: Croydon Airport in the 1950s was popular with flying clubs and as a base for local maintenance companies such as Rollasons, and here an impressive line-up of planes and vehicles stand on the tarmac in front of the terminal *(facing page, top)*.

Croydon Aerodrome was established back in 1915 for military use during World War I. After the war, a civil airport was established and work began on converting the wartime hangars and buildings and former military aircraft to peacetime civil use. Business, though slow at first, eventually picked up as links were forged with overseas clients around Europe.

Air travel was in its infancy as far as the ordinary holidaymaker was concerned, and only the most adventurous dreamed of forsaking the deck chairs of Southend and Brighton for unknown foreign shores and unfamiliar food. In 1928 a brand new terminal transformed Croydon into an ultra-modern airport, and the increase in traffic was spectacular as it became a destination for the major airlines of Europe. Lufthansa and Air France were among the many airlines whose aircraft were regularly seen on the tarmac at Croydon; the busy scene above shows a Lufthansa Condor Focke-Wulf

D-AMHC complete with swastika tail markings, with two Air France Bloch 220 aircraft behind. This scene was captured during the 1930s, and before many months had passed the Lufthansa and its swastika would no longer be welcomed in Croydon.

Throughout the second world war Croydon was used as a fighter base, with Spitfires, Hurricanes and Wellingtons dominating the skies above the town. When peace was declared in 1945, the airport successfully readjusted to civil flying and it remained busy. Even so, the end of the road was unfortunately already in sight for Croydon. Heathrow Airport, which had opened in 1946, was better equipped to take larger aircraft such as the Constellation, Hermes, Stratocruiser and the DC-4, and Croydon was left behind in the bid for international custom. The photograph on the right, taken by John Caston, Croydon Times' chief photographer on Wednesday May 28th 1958, is probably the last picture of Croydon Airport. A couple of days later Transair Ltd began to transfer planes to Gatwick, and on 9th June the announcement was made that as Croydon Airport was too small for the needs of modern airlines it would close at the end of September 1959.

Shopping spree

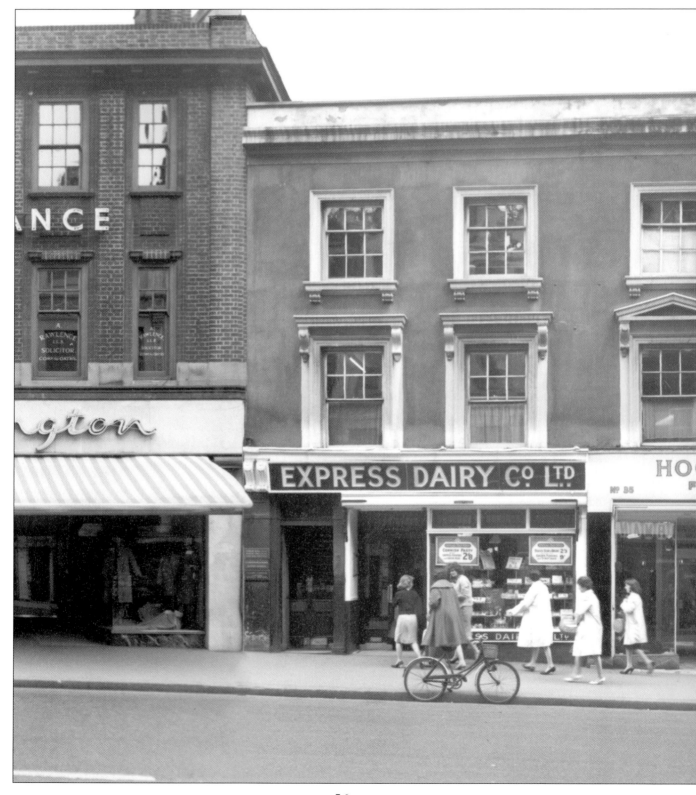

The Croydon was a popular Croydon watering hole back in 1960; how many readers remember whiling away the odd evening in Batty's Bar? Built at the turn of the 20th century, The Croydon became an institution in the town until it became the Rat and Parrot in 1994. The 'square block' architecture of the mid 20th century was to eventually replace this beautiful building. Hockley's Furriers adjoined the hotel; back in 1960, the date of this memorable photograph, they were only one of several in the town, and the possession of a fur coat was still a fashion statement among the more affluent. By the end of the decade, however, certain groups of people were beginning to swing the tide of public opinion against the wearing of genuine fur. That was when 'fun fur' came into vogue, and some of our lady readers will no doubt remember with nostalgia the 'ocelot' or 'ermine' that they wore during the 1970s. These fake furs might have been cheap but they were not regarded as 'tacky'. Stylish, affordable - and a political statement - the fun to wear furs could be seen everywhere. We cannot let the opportunity pass of mentioning the Express Dairy, sadly non-existent today. A sign in the window reminds us that more than dairy produce was sold here - their Cornish pasties were selling for 2/8d.

By kind permission of the Croydon Advertiser Group

Croydon Local Studies Library

A solitary car makes its way along High Street in this view from 1950, yet we notice that the pavements on either side of the road are crowded with pedestrians. For those who were in need of public transport to get them home, the tram lines remind us that Croydon still had trams at the time - though not for very much longer. Less than a year after the photograph, the last of the old trams left Croydon bound for that great tram shed in the sky. The tram was raided, before its departure, by hordes of souvenir hunters, who took away with them everything they could lay their hands on, even if it was nailed down! How many of the crews'

A glance at the 1950s

WHAT'S ON?

Television hit Britain in a big way during the 1950s. Older readers will surely remember 'Double Your Money', 'Dixon of Dock Green' and 'Dragnet' (whose characters' names were changed 'to protect the innocent'). Commercial television was introduced on 22nd September 1955, and Gibbs SR toothpaste were drawn out of the hat to become the first advert to be shown. Many believed adverts to be vulgar, however, and audiences were far less than had been hoped for.

GETTING AROUND

The year 1959 saw the development of the world's first practical air-cushion vehicle - better known to us as the hovercraft. The earliest model was only able to travel at slow speeds over very calm water and was unable to carry more than three passengers. The faster and smoother alternative to the sea ferry quickly caught on, and by the 1970s a 170-ton car-carrying hovercraft service had been introduced across the English Channel.

SPORTING CHANCE

The four-minute mile had remained the record since 1945, and had become regarded as virtually unbreakable. On 6th May 1954, however, Oxford University student Roger Bannister literally ran away with the record, accomplishing the seemingly impossible in three minutes 59.4 seconds. Bannister collapsed at the end of his last amazing lap, even temporarily losing his vision. By the end of the day, however, he had recovered sufficiently to celebrate his achievement in a London night club!

uniform jackets, seats, destination blinds, lamps, and handrails are still tucked away, half forgotten, in box rooms and lofts around Croydon? All those guilty, wave your tram drivers' caps.... Several of the drivers and crews from the old trams would be invited to attend the launch of the town's new Tramlink system, which was to officially open late in 1999.

A little piece of Croydon's history - Crown Hill as it was in June 1938 - and two-way traffic, crowds of pedestrians, shop windows overflowing with goods, and fascinating advertising hoardings all add their own distinctive flavour to the scene. Many readers will have their own special memories of evenings spent at the Hippodrome, which was further down the hill on the right. The Hippodrome, previously the Theatre Royal, opened as a variety theatre back in 1910 and was given over to films eight years later. It was in 1929, however, when it made history in

Croydon as the first cinema outside the West End to install the equipment needed to screen talking pictures. Back in the 1920s 'talkies' were the wonder technology of the day, and on 4th February 1929 cinemagoers crowded into Croydon to hear a singing and talking Al Jolson in 'The Singing Fool'. That first week, 19,017 people came to shed romantic tears over Jolson's rendering of 'Danny Boy', which became everyone's favourite song. The Hippodrome - which had already been bought by British Home Stores - closed on 3rd November 1956.

The Allders Collection

Above: The reason behind this kiddies' attraction in Allders' department store has been lost in the mist of time, but this Submarine Trip to Father Neptune certainly proved popular with the children. A busy background of biplanes flying high over the ocean, and the sleek outline of an airship (which at the time promised to be the transport of the future), sets the scene. We can imagine what a thrill awaited these youngsters as they paid their sixpences and entered the door at the top of the stairway, then descended to Neptune's green and shimmering world at the bottom of the sea.

The great god of the sea himself, trident in hand, would be waiting there to greet them, possibly with a mermaid or two, modestly dressed of course, in attendance. An assortment of well-dentured sharks and robust octopuses with lengthy tentacles would no doubt have formed part of the exciting background, pleasing the little boys and horrifying their sisters. We have no date for the photograph, but it captures for us those long ago, computer-free days, when children enjoyed life and its simpler pleasures.

Above right: When this scene of change was snapped in the 1920s, Allders had already been trading in Croydon for around 60 years. Little had changed since the days when Joshua Allder had expanded his business into adjoining shops back in the late 19th century, and now it was time for a facelift that would link North End and George Street by means of an arcade. Haskins is the firm carrying out the rebuilding programme, but other notices

The Allders Collection

posted above the well stocked displays are not so easily read. Wouldn't it be fascinating to gaze into the windows and discover just what bargains in shirts, ties and jackets were on offer? Allders' Mall is as fascinating today, and shoppers can browse in undercover comfort among a huge choice of goods. With a large selection of cheeses, delicatessen, Belgian chocolate, travel goods, specialist coffee and modern communications, whether you want to buy a money belt, a briefcase or half a pound of blue Stilton, you will find it in Allders' Mall.

This page: Christmas, as the large sign shouts at passers by *(below)* just glitters at Allders, and with the department store already established, at the time of the photograph, as one of Croydon's major stores, you could buy everything on your Christmas present list all under one roof. With windows ablaze with light, illuminated signs and Bethlehem stars guiding people to spend their cash at Allders, what prospective Santa Claus could resist filling his sack here? After Christmas, of course, would come the January sales, when Father Christmas's leftovers would be snapped up by thrifty Croydonians who had queued outside the doors hoping to find a bargain *(bottom)*. Interestingly, a few decades on in 1986, the tills would ring up that magic £1m on the very first day of the winter sale. Croydon's favourite store, today the third largest department store in Britain, was established by Joshua Allder back in 1862.

Incredibly, he was just 24 years of age when he took on two shops in North End and opened up specialising in silks and linen drapery. Under his guiding hand, the business proved to be a runaway success, and after Mr Allders' retirement in 1902 the firm changed hands. In the 1920s, an extensive renovation and rebuilding programme was undertaken - work which the Luftwaffe did their best to undo in World War II. Though the flying bomb and incendiaries did a lot of damage, Allders came through the war able to claim proudly, 'we never closed'.

The Allders Collection

Left: The many open windows tell us that Croydon is enjoying a warm day. Shoppers are out in full force in their light summery clothes, and a mother has raised the hood of her pram to protect her baby from the hot sun. A sharp eye will spot the gentleman on his second floor balcony above Courlander's jeweller's on the left. In those less casual days he would not be seen in public, of course, in his shirt sleeves and braces - but who is going to raise their eyes from street level and see him up there? With wild daring this gentleman has removed his jacket - and possibly even his collar and tie, and with his back to the street he little knows that a photographer stands below, camera at the ready, to capture the revealing little scene for all time....

The names above the shops will evoke many memories. Edmonds Wools, for example, who interestingly for the 1940s bought directly from the mills; perhaps their stock was brought up from Bradford, centre of the woollen industry at the time? Freeman, Hardy and Willis, too, were a well known chain of shoe shops back then. When, exactly, did the company's name disappear from the streets of Britain? The hairdresser's shop above Courlander's offers Marcel waving, indicating the 1940s as the time of the photograph.

Below: Young mothers with prams and toddlers, housewives with baskets - all needed to top up the larder with fresh produce in the days when few kitchens could boast a refrigerator, and many of them would have already paid a visit to Sainsbury's in Church Street, seen here on the left. The grocery chain already had three or four shops around Croydon at the time, and a few decades on were to become the well known super-store giants.

Though a couple of gentlemen are finding something fascinating to gaze at (photographic equipment perhaps?), the windows of Boots chemists shop were nevertheless rather dull when we compare them with the chemist's shops of today, that sparkle with jewellery, hair ornaments, cameras and cosmetics. This was the place to go, however, not only to have your films developed and your doctor's medicines dispensed but to buy the popular home remedies that had stood the test of time: castor oil, ipecacuanha, camphorated oil, Indian Brandee and Fennings fever powders.

Croydon Local Studies Library

Above: Christmas shopping; you either love it or hate it - but you still have to do it! Every shop you enter glitters with tinsel, Christmas trees and gifts, but it's after dark that Croydon comes to brilliant life with hundreds of coloured lights that sparkle like gemstones in the darkness. This spectacular view of Grants department store, decorated for a long-ago Christmas, was taken on Christmas Eve, 1966. The well-known store, established in Croydon in 1877, had every-thing for the gift-seeker, from fashions to sports and travel goods. Grants closed in the early 1980s.

In today's commercially-minded society, Christmas trees, coloured lights and elaborate decorations find their way into the shops around the end of September, along with the endless gifts we are expected to spend hundreds of pounds on. We would not wish for a return to the poverty that marked the early years of the 20th century, when Santa left few if any gifts in children's stockings - but oh, for a return to those simple, non-material-istic Christmases!

Right: Surrey Street Market had the same kind of life and energy back in the 1960s as it still enjoys today, when we are able to buy a wider range of products than ever before.

The market, selling mainly fruit and vegetables, has always had a character of its very own, and many local housewives, who love a bargain as much as anyone else, have made a beeline for this spot for many years. Week after week Croydonians would catch a bus into town and tour the market to find the best - and cheapest - apples, pears, oranges, grapefruit and bananas. Buying potatoes and tomatoes from one stall, apples and sprouts from another and perhaps cabbage and a couple of avocado pears from a third have always been part of the fun of bargain hunting in the market. The prices charged by markets and street traders have traditionally been a few coppers cheaper than the average high street greengrocer would charge, and a weekly walk through the market - especially at the end of the day - could stretch the inadequate housekeeping money a little bit further. Today you might browse along Surrey Street and find stalls offering nothing but avocados or perhaps eggs.

The John Gent Collection

This view of Lower Church Street was captured on a day of summer sunshine in July 1959. The scene will be only partially familiar to younger readers, as the buildings in the distance no longer exist today. Many smaller businesses such as Broomfields and Taylors were once a common sight around Croydon. Sadly, many of them are gone, together with the personal service we once took for granted. Small grocery chains and corner butchers were the traditional way to shop, and we would queue to be served while the butcher cubed our stewing steak and cut our sausages from a long string hanging above the counter. The grocer would weigh out goods such as biscuits, sugar, dried fruit and salt and pepper for the individual customer - a far cry from today's plastic packs! People might have had to wait a while longer to be served, but at least they had the benefit of personal attention from the staff. At the time of the photograph self-service shopping had already begun to catch on. The trend started slowly, but it was the thin end of the wedge. Over the last forty or so years we have moved inexorably towards super- and hyper-markets and out of town shopping.

At work

Croydon Local Studies Library

It was 21st January 1936, and these three police officers look remarkably cheerful considering that they had just returned from the scene of a motor bike crash in London Road; it was obviously not a serious one. We have been unable to unearth any details of this particular crash, which did not appear to have made the local newspaper. Its cause, however, in those pre-breathalyser days when the smell of alcohol on the breath was all the police had to go on, could have been similar to a case heard in court that same week. A motor cyclist who crashed into the side of a car was convicted for dangerous driving on 6th July; he successfully appealed against his conviction and instead, the tide of suspicion turned towards the driver of the car, who had swerved directly into the cyclist's path just a quarter of an hour after leaving a local hostelry. When questioned, the driver vehemently denied that the three double whiskies he had drunk during the evening had influenced his driving in any way....

Enormous changes are afoot as workmen crack on with the construction of Fairfield underground car park in Park Lane. Piled up girders, stepladders, lengths of piping and all the paraphernalia of a construction site add an atmosphere of busyness, while workmen, cement mixer, lifting gear and lorries complete this scene of Croydon's progress. Just beyond, we can make out the line of the underpass which is just taking shape. The scene - captured in June 1963 from the top of the Technical College - also takes in St George's House which was

being constructed at the time, adding more new shops and offices to Croydon's facilities. The 'new' Greyhound pub stands nearby, while further along park Lane we can see the headquarters of the South Eastern Gas Board - doomed to stand empty by the late 1990s. Croydon's first gas works was established in Butcher Row in 1827, and readers might find their prices interesting; the cost of outdoor lamps kept burning from dusk to daylight, inclusive of attendance and lighting, was £7.7s per annum - which was payable quarterly.

Below: A cloud of dust rises above the rubble as the last walls of The Greyhound give way to the onslaught of the bulldozers, and a moment in Croydon's history is captured on film for all time. The workmen, we know, were there to do a job, but how many of them watched the last moments of the old pub with a tinge of sadness? The Greyhound had a history that could be traced back to the 17th century, when some of Fairfax's soldiers put up at The Greyhound during the Civil War, and an inn of the same name, which incidentally brewed its own beer, was referred to as early as 1493. In the 1800s The Greyhound had a ballroom where monthly balls were held after every full moon, reminding us of the dangers that lurked on the dark and lonely roads back then. The pub has a connection, too, with 20th century history, having been used by Sir Arthur Conan Doyle during a stay in Croydon.

A clear view of the Town Hall was, and still is, an unaccustomed sight from this viewpoint, as St George's Walk shopping precinct was to eventually replace the old Greyhound.

Making sure there are always plenty of good things in store for Croydon...

Life in Croydon just wouldn't be the same without Allders. We wouldn't know where to buy things from; we would miss having a browse round on a Saturday; we would be stuck for ideas at Christmas; we would miss its sales; and some of us would be short of a job. Of course there was a time when Allders did not exist; it is difficult for us to imagine, but then it is hard for us to picture what Croydon was like, prior to 1862.

The Croydon of the mid 19th century was a small town, quite separate from London. The journey from Croydon to London would have taken the traveller through a series of small villages, separated by green fields; a very different journey from today, when the villages have merged together into suburban South London. So when Mr Joshua Allder, born at 11 Upper Garden Street, Walworth on May 2nd, 1838, left his South London home at the age of 16 and set out to become an apprentice to Charles Messent, hosier, of Croydon, it was quite a brave move. It is thought that Joshua's family had at one

Right: *A delivery vehicle circa 1920.* **Below:** *The store in the very early days.*

stage been shopkeepers in Northumberland; there are records of a Caleb Allder having a shop in Newcastle where he sold 'cheeses, bacon, ham, herrings, oranges, nuts and apples'. Joshua, however, favoured silks; after finishing his apprenticeship he took over two shops, numbers 102 and 103 North End, and set himself up, in 1862, as a 'linen draper and silk mercer'.

Around this time shopping habits underwent a gradual change. Previously it had been the custom for the

tradesman to either visit the houses of his customers personally, or to send his wares by delivery boy, according to the nature of the transaction; or, if the customer did drive into town, he would not enter the shop but would wait outside in the street in his carriage, and the shopkeeper would take the goods out to him. In the course of the 19th century, however, it became gradually more accepted for customers to go inside shops.

Above: An elegant Ladies' Daywear Department in the 1930s. **Below:** *The store decked out for the Coronation of HM Queen Elizabeth in 1953.*

Joshua Allder's business opened in 1862, with a special introductory offer of silk dresses at £5 each. No doubt many Victorian ladies were tempted into his shop by this offer, but Joshua Allder was too shrewd to rely on the whims of the ladies for his business. He, along with many other successful mercers of the time, knew that whilst a lady may or may not allow herself to indulge in a new silk dress, she would almost certainly at some stage be obliged to dress in mourning; as the Victorians were unfailingly strict in their observance of the custom of wearing black throughout the mourning period. So Joshua's shop had a department which sold special mourning garb. Then

he had another department which sold ribbons, and one which sold buttons; so the ladies who had treated themselves to a new outfit could add the finishing touches in the form of matching decorations, while those who had denied themselves could console themselves here with new ribbons and bows to brighten up an old gown or hat.

In the latter part of the 19th century Croydon became a favourite place for young people to come and seek their fortune; and as the population of the town increased, so did trade. Joshua Allder began to acquire neighbouring properties as they became available, and before very long his business occupied numbers 102, 103, 104, 106 and 107 North End, and consisted of drapery and linen departments, household furnishings and a carpet warehouse. Unfortunately number 105 North End was owned by a baker, who showed no inclination to move; and not until some 20 years later was Joshua able to complete his chain of shops along the east side of North End. Mr Allder himself lived in Whitehorse Road with his wife and family; he had married a Staffordshire lady named Miss Jane Colclough. Universally respected by those who knew him, he was a man of strong religious convictions, and also a very caring man; he had a genuine concern for his employees, and took a leading role in civic affairs. A well-known and respected local figure, he was elected a member of the Local Board of Health in 1881, and following Croydon's incorporation by Charter - something for which Mr Allder and other leading shopkeepers of the town had campaigned vigorously - he was elected representative for the West ward in the first Borough Council elections, held on 1st June 1885. In all, he was Alderman for nine years. He was also a prominent member of the Chamber of Commerce and a founder member, director and for a time Chairman of the Croydon Tramway Company; and he did all he could to assist Catherine Booth, the wife of Reverend William Booth, when she came to Croydon to set up a Salvation Army Mission.

As an employer, Joshua Allder took his responsibil-

Right: *A Royal Tableau performed by Allders' staff in the 1930s.*
Below: *Shoppers outside Allders in the early 1960s.*

ities very seriously. Many of his staff lived above the premises, now called Commerce House, and Joshua paid great attention to their morals and welfare. He also supported the campaign for shorter working hours for shopworkers, becoming Treasurer of the Croydon Early Closing Association. Most shops at that time were open every day except Sunday from seven o'clock in the morning until nine o'clock at night in summer, and half-past seven or eight o'clock in the winter. Sunday was a day of rest, and occasionally a Saint's day was declared a holiday. Occasionally a member of staff at Allders enjoyed a rather unusual break from their normal duties - they were appointed to ride on the tram between Thornton Heath and Purley, as ticket inspectors (their employer a member of the Tramway Company). It was thanks to pressure exerted by Mr Allder and the

such a
wonderful
place for —
CHRISTMAS
SHOPPING

ALLDERS

Croydon Early Closing Association that the big shops began to close early on a Wednesday; at first this simply took the form of releasing the assistants at five o'clock, and it developed into the tradition of half-day closing. Allders is thought to have begun closing on a Wednesday afternoon in 1870, although two o'clock closing was not generally introduced until February 1896.

By the turn of the 20th century an extensive department store had grown up, with Joshua's original premises at numbers 102 and 103 now being filled by the China & Glass department alone. Allders was respected as a large and important business, and its founder was regarded as 'a steadying power in North End'. Having retired from politics in 1891, in 1902 he moved with his family to a new house on the Haling estate in Pampisford Road. Two years later he died suddenly after a heart attack. He was buried at Queen's Road Cemetery and the service was held at the West Croydon Tabernacle - many mourners braved the torrential rain to pay their final respects to a fine, upright citizen with 'a genius for business'.

Allders store was sold in 1908 to Messrs J W Holdron and F C Bearman who kept the business until 1921, by which time it was organised into some 50 departments and employed a staff of 500. It subsequently remained in the hands of the Lawrence family for many years, becoming a limited company with first Daniel Lawrence and then his son John as managing director. Extensive

Above: The store facade decked out for Christmas in the 1950s.

building works were carried out during the 1920s and 30s. The first Arcade, developed in 1925, proved a great attraction, and in 1932 the stables at the rear of the premises were demolished and another Arcade was built to link North End with George Street. The impressive North End facade was constructed around 1926. Allders, with its progressive approach to retailing, continued to make the headlines; in June 1933 an advertisement in the Croydon Advertiser exhorted readers to visit the Allders 1933 Bungalow during Festival Week. Situated on the store roof, this exhibition consisted of an 'All Electric Home with its Beautiful Gardens', and readers were assured that they would 'be charmed with the many labour-saving devices, but on no account will be pressed to make purchases'.

Unfortunately a considerable amount of damage occurred during the second world war, with the main staircase being completely demolished when Allders suffered a direct hit; however, the staff, led by managing director Daniel Lawrence, kept the store open throughout the war in spite of the structural damage and the difficult trading conditions, and afterwards were proud to be able to boast, 'We never closed'. Post-war modernisations to the premises included the installation of the first thermal air curtain door in Croydon and the first escalators in Croydon - in 1954. Allders was still in competition with Croydon's other two large department stores, Grants and Kennards (now Debenhams), but of the three it was Allders' expansion and capacity for innovation which was to set it apart. In 1952 the Scala cinema was purchased and the auditorium became Allders' new Hardware and Gift Hall. The following year John Lawrence took the business over following his father's death, but five years later - mainly as a result of crippling death duties - the store was taken over by the United Drapery Stores Group, who kept John on as managing director. Shortly afterwards plans to demolish the old Scala cinema and create a four-floor store were put into effect.

Annual turnover reached the million mark in 1958, the year it became part of the United Drapery Stores Group, and by 1963 this figure had trebled. Part of the reason for this rapid increase in turnover was a shift in emphasis within the store, with the Household departments taking precedence over Fashion. The store continued to grow throughout the 60s and early 70s; the George Street premises of the House of Savage were acquired upon the retirement of Mr Savage in February 1960, and a five-year construction project was begun in 1965 and culminated in Croydon's Whitgift Centre. Allders now had shop fronts on North End, Dingwall Avenue, George Street and in the Centre itself. By 1976 further building work had created an additional 220,000 square feet of floor space, at a cost of some three and three-quarter million pounds. Allders, already the premier store and a landmark in its own right in Croydon, was now the third largest department store in

the United Kingdom (after Harrods and Selfridges), with a total floor space of more than 500,000 square feet and a staff of around 1,700.

Lifestyle changes in the latter part of the 20th century had led to a more mobile population with more leisure time to travel further afield; Allders' most intense competition now came not from the local shops but

Right: The Ladies' Department in the late 1950s.
Below: A well stocked Haberdashery.

from the West End stores. Nineteen eighty-four saw the beginning of a major programme to update many areas of the store including Menswear, China & Glass, the Fashion Floor, and Perfumery and Fashion Accessories; the Perfumery Hall was equipped with a beauty room for private consultations with consultants from the world's top cosmetic and perfumery houses. The addition of a completely new floor on top of the existing building began three years later; this new 20,000 square foot Fourth Floor extension, high above the rooftops, became the home of two restaurants and the Audio & Television Department.

A succession of management changes took place during the 1980s. The UDS Group of companies was acquired by Hanson plc in 1983; and in 1989 a successful management buy-out bid resulted in Allders Department Stores and its sister company Allders International becoming an independant company, Allders Limited. This company subsequently became Allders plc following a successful flotation on the Stock Exchange in 1993.

The major refurbishment of the Whitgift Centre which began in the Spring of 1994 will still be relatively fresh in the minds of readers. Some £4 million was spent on the refurbishment of Perfumery, Fashion Accessories and Carpets, and a new store frontage was created in the square adjacent to the Store, now appropriately known as Allders Square. Canopied by a fantastic glass atrium and equipped with a new escalator and glass

elevator, this quickly became a great talking-point and attracted shoppers from a wide area.

Croydon today is proud of its excellent and attractive shopping facilities, and with good reason; Allders provides everything for the shopper of the new millennium. The store's growth in size and popularity is a credit to Mr Joshua Allder who founded a solid business on sound business principles almost 140 years ago, and to all those who have worked to ensure its continued success in the years which followed. Croydon's best-known store will continue to serve Croydon's shoppers for many, many years to come.

Above: *The Toy and Children's Department.*
Below: *The store celebrating its 108th birthday.*

Going Dutch, the Philips way

The giant Philips concern in the Netherlands has arms that reach across the world. It even formed its own major professional soccer team, PSV Eindhoven. For a number of years the former England manager, Bobby Robson, coached the side to both domestic and European success. A leading name in the electrical business, it came to Britain in 1925 as Philips Lamps Ltd. However, it was not until 1956 that a large new TV factory came to Croydon. To call it just a factory is hardly doing it justice. It was almost the size of a small village, in itself. Over two thirds of a mile of overhead conveyor systems kept the work flowing in a seemingly never ending supply. With this arrangement there was little need for storage at floor level. The work was circulated in a continuous sweep of cabinets, circuit boards and assorted parts. At different stages of the journey the conveyors would suddenly swoop down to a lower level. Like hungry birds demanding to be fed, they would be asking for the loading or removal of pieces of equipment that were necessary to the next stage in the production process. Then the conveyors would soar again to move on to the next 'feeding station'. There were six of these systems that constantly hummed and rattled their way through the day, each and every shift on each and every working day. It was an exercise in careful planning and effective delivery that gave the desired result - efficient production. Powered roller conveyors carried the TV cabinets half a mile down the line to the waiting final assembly point. Here the sets that would bear the proud name of Philips would receive their last inspection. Then it was off to the packing and despatch area as another batch of TVs went to the homes of children anxious to see the antics of Muffin the Mule and the programmes that were coming from the new wonder kid, ITV.

It was a time when the buzz of the valves as they warmed in the set made us sit in anticipation of what was in store for us on the 'gogglebox'. Soon the velvety tones of Richard Dimbleby or the tuneful playing of Shirley Abicair's zither would be coming from within the box. In an age of slipping horizontal hold and 425 lines, Philips was always striving to keep ahead of its competitors and bring new, faster and more reliable technology into the world of electrical engineering. Always with one eye on Ferguson, its main rival, the Philips company kept a year or two ahead of the others in the 1950s. The use of the printed circuit board (PCB) was one such development. The Americans had used printed circuits for fuses in anti-aircraft shells. It had also put them into the cockpits of aeroplanes, using them in the vast array of on board electronic instruments. Transferring their use into domestic appliances was a natural progression. It is reassuring to see that the spin-off from war and its machines can sometimes have beneficial effects in peacetime. The

Below: *Philips Service, 604 Purley Way, Croydon circa 1955.*

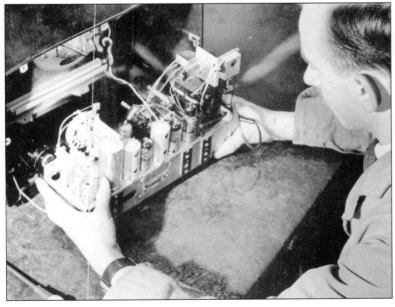

Production continued to grow in Croydon in the swinging 60s as people had more and more money in their pockets. Televisions became a necessary part of any household furniture. As it became standard to own a fridge, a vacuum cleaner and a washing machine, we realised that the day of the electrical age was firmly with us. Heated hair rollers took the place of the old-fashioned 'manual' ones and pop stars plugged in their guitars, rather than strumming them. During this period, and into the 1970s, there was a British feel to the design of the Philips TV sets. Most people wanted a relatively cheap, but reliable, receiver. Fiddly or ornate refinements were not needed. Those designed in Eindhoven had a greater continental flavour. The Dutch, Germans and French went for high-spec, we went for basics. The British attitude was that you can fill your stomach with fish and chips just as easily as paté de foie gras. 'Softly, softly' or the 'Liver Birds' looked just as good in a conventional cabinet as one with extra twiddly bits and a few extra sockets and buttons. In 1976, Philips took over Pye completely. A detailed study was made of their respective television receivers, leading to the development of the G11 chassis.

In 1980 the delivery of colour television receivers by the industry was almost 2 million, despite rising unemployment and high interest rates. However, Philips at both their television factories were

space probes and rockets to the moon have given us the chance to experiment and test before adapting the ideas into a useful tool for the consumer. Scientists, with their thoughts turned to solving problems created by high temperatures, were scratching their heads at Philips, as the use of the PCBs gave problems. The tags of the valve holders inside the TV sets regularly overheated. So hot did they become that even the solder melted and the board would be damaged. Using expertise learned in the handling of elements at fierce temperatures, the problem was solved by the use of copper that took the heat away from the valves. So, the more advanced 'innards' of the TV could be fitted and greater reliability guaranteed.

Above left: Removing a Philips radio chassis from its cabinet for service - circa 1955. **Top:** *Servicing a Philips television receiver - circa 1955.*

producing well below capacity and the former Pye factory at Lowestoft, which in the early 1970s employed 2,800 people, was closed with the loss of 1,100 jobs. Philips concentrated the manufacture of television receivers at the Croydon works which was entirely refurbished. In 1984 it was described as a "member of the network of Philips European CTV factories", having a workforce of 1,200 and the capacity to produce 500,000 colour receivers annually. Sadly, redundancies began in 1985 and only 500 workers were left when it closed in December 1988. Production was moved to a Philips factory in Bruges, Belgium.

It is always sad to see a landmark disappear or a symbol of one's youth go forever. After being around for years, suddenly this branch of the Philips empire was no more. It was not long before it was followed by Philips Service that had premises at 604 Purley Way. This organisation could trace back its origins in Croydon to before the second world war. Having come to Britain as a part of the lighting industry, the Company moved into the electronics field in 1928 when it began distributing radio receivers, loudspeakers and similar goods. These all came from the factories of the parent company in the Netherlands. The BBC had only been on air for a few years and the radio business was still in its infancy. Inside the sets the valves used a high level of electric current. Heavy accumulators had to be used and these needed recharging at the local garage every few days or so. Imagine lugging your radio to the nearest Texaco twice a week! There was an opening for someone who could develop a plug in radio that ran off the mains. Philips stepped in. By 1930, it had several models that did just that. No other manufacturer could offer a similar set. Retailing at around £28 for an average mains radio, the Philips name was soon in many of the living rooms of the nation. Family life had changed. Before long, it would be a common sight for mum, dad and the kids to cluster round the 'wireless' and enjoy the varied entertainment coming along the airwaves.

Below: London Carriers vehicle - circa 1949.
Bottom: London Carriers vehicle - circa 1955. All the vehicles on these pages were a familiar sight around Croydon.

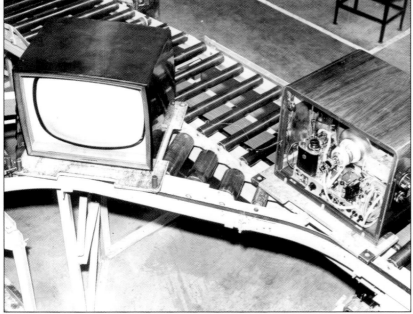

radios for even the tiniest of repairs, so as not to invalidate the guarantee. Philips changed the policy and, from 1931, allowed other dealers to carry out the repairs. In 1930, a service and inspection centre had been set up in Mitcham. But, in 1937, the Service Department moved to Croydon. On Waddon Factory Estate, near Croydon Airport, large modern workshops were built. These were badly damaged in the Blitz of 1940 and staff were relocated to the centre of the town. During the war, much work was carried out for the Air Ministry. Aircraft transmitters and receivers gave the Service Department plenty of work to keep them occupied. With this support, the Department was able to rebuild the Waddon premises and move back in by the time hostilities ended.

In the decade after the war the service load increased rapidly, partly due to the expansion of television and partly due to a much wider range of merchandise sold not only under the Philips brand name but by a growing number of associated companies.

In the early 1960s the service organisation faced a new task when the range of products sold by the Philips

There was little in the way of specialised radio dealing or repairs . Bike shops and garages seemed to be places where you got the radio servicing done. Philips' sets were sold with a guarantee, but there was a catch. The repairs had to be carried out by Philips personnel in a Company workshop. It was essential to set up such a centre in Britain. People would hardly buy a product they had to send overseas should it need repairing. A small centre was established near London Bridge in late 1928. This and other small centres could not cope with the amount of work that followed. Owners returned

Above left: *Faulty sets are diverted from the production line in 1957.*
Top: *London Carriers vehicle - circa 1952.*

Group was extended to include major domestic appliances such as washing machines, spin dryers and refrigerators. It was now necessary to provide throughout the country a team of mobile service engineers with fully equipped vans that were supported, at strategic points, by small provincial depots.

A training school was established at the Purley Way premises, where dealers could send their engineers for free specialised training in servicing Philips Group products. Philips Service continued to be in Purley Way until this organisation closed in 1990.

Throughout these years, the Philips transport organisation of London Carriers Ltd had developed along parallel lines. In more modern times, it dealt with insurance and travel agency, as well as the transport business with which it first began. The financial side came about in 1968, when London and World Insurance Brokers, later L & O Insurance Brokers, became a London Carriers' subsidiary. It provided insurance services to the whole of the Philips Group. Being close to Lloyds, it was at the heart of the global market. By the 1970s, the travel agency had been added. This served both Philips' staff and the general public. All this time, the silver vans of London Carriers, driven by men in smart Philips blue uniforms, were providing the same sort of continuous service as given by those conveyor

Above: *Philips' Croydon works in 1957.*

systems in the Croydon factory. From factory floor to the High Street shop, radios, televisions, hi-fis and much more would be winging their way to satisfied customers. Eagerly unpacking their new purchase back home, those customers would not have spared a thought for the carrier who had so carefully and reliably brought that prized possession to them. He was not worried. He was already off down the motorway with another delivery.

It had all started in 1927, the days of the flapper and prohibition. Philips Lamps could not find anyone who could give steady service as a shipping agent. Chancing on the newly formed London Carriers, a long-lasting marriage was made. Increased activity saw the company move to bigger and bigger premises several times in the first few years. By 1936, the operation had moved to Waddon, so keeping the marriage even closer together. After the war, the administration section moved from London to Waddon and, in 1958, to Scarbrook Road, Croydon. The transport services took advantage of the booming economy of the late 1950s and 1960s. Just like Topsy, the business 'just growed'. Premises were acquired in Nottingham and Birmingham followed in 1960. Two years later, the sensible move was made to rent part of a building at London Airport. This gave easy access to one of the busiest freight handling spots in the world. In the same way, the 1969 opening at Harwich, British Railway's largest container depot, was a sound choice. By 1971, Heywood and Cambridge also saw bases for London Carriers. By then, there were 350 commercial vehicles and 3,000 company cars on the road. As the Philips Group refocused in the 1990s, so this bridal partner had to adjust. However, London Carriers Ltd was sold in 1990.

Since the dark days between the wars, Philips has brought a little light to the workers and shoppers of Croydon. It is apt that it was as Philips Lamps that we made our first acquaintance.

Left: *A television tube is loaded into a cradle transported by the overhead conveyor - 1957.*
Below: *Close to the conveyor, the monorail drops to allow tubes to be fitted to cabinets - 1957.*

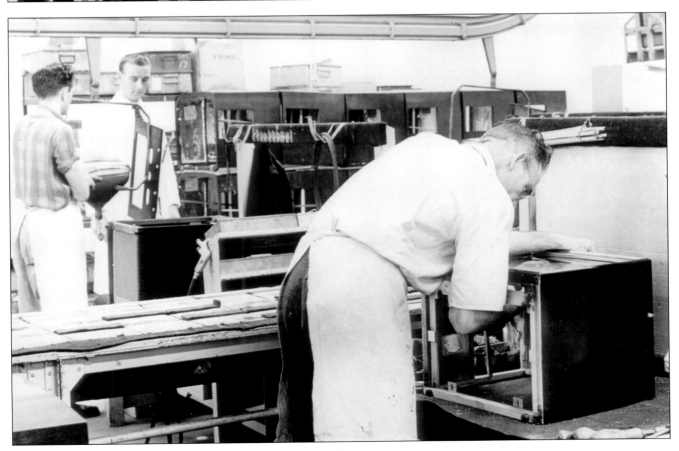

Integrity and excellence at all levels

Many a business has been founded on the basis of a chance accident leading to a career change. Frederick Goodliffe had formerly been a partner in a shipping company trading with the Cape Colony and Natal until war with the two Boer republics disrupted trade. As a family man before the days of Social Security he had to find work and so he joined The Great International Window Cleaning Company of Holborn as a canvasser on ten bob a week plus commission. He left this grandiloquently titled firm after a dispute over his pay and, in 1900, founded the well named New Century Window and General Cleaning Company.

With the aid of a part timer the firm, whose single hand cart, ladder and pail were parked overnight in a pub yard, operated from over a sweet shop to capture business in the mighty City of London. The business grew to employ ten window cleaners by 1911 to be joined by the fourteen year old Gilbert Goodliffe as office boy a year later. Following the 1918 Armistice nephew Bert Westwood started as office boy on twenty five bob (£1.25p) a week to retire as Managing director in 1968. This set the pattern for a tradition of long service and family involvement in a company that has provided new services to meet changing demands.

Up until the late thirties business houses employed their own cleaners-cum-caretakers who lived in small flats above their workplaces. It had once been common for shop staff to live in and obey restrictions on their social lives! The prejudice against employing outsiders to clean premises after hours was slowly changing as the redoubtable Mrs Mops gave way to cleaning companies such as Frederick Goodliffe's Office Cleaning Services. A bank which feared that his cleaners might steal their carpets actually called on OCS, in 1939, to shift its bullion! From the beginning the firm advertised that its staff were fully insured against accidents. Looking at photographs of the wooden ladders extending to the fourth floor of office buildings it is easy to see why customers were attracted by this policy.

New Century pioneered holiday pay for cleaners in the late 1920s and bought its first van in 1930. During World War Two the firm found itself cleaning the Underground Railway stations, used in the London 'Blitz' as overnight accommodation, and even expanding its office cleaning with reduced staff. Bombed out itself the firm made do in an overcrowded temporary office when 'Business as Usual' was the national motto.

The post-war years saw rapid expansion as key staff returned to 'civvy street' to rebuild old contacts and to develop new leads and methods, materials and equipment. It is still company policy to reward any of its staff who successfully introduce new business. The Dulwich Hamlet Football Club, which asked if OCS did laundry, prompted the purchase of Bill Smart's Laundry, in 1956, to complete the circle started by 'The Guv'nor', Fred Goodliffe, who as a boy had worked in the family laundry. Unfortunately he had died nine years earlier a few years before either the Eagle Street offices were built or the move south of the Thames to Vauxhall.

Today OCS Group is the largest privately owned property support services company based in the United Kingdom. Through its network of over 40 trading subsidiaries operating from some 250

Top left: *Frederick Goodliffe, "The Guv'nor" in 1946.*
Above: *An estimate for cleaning the new Daily Mail building, Carmelite House from 1927. The estimate was successful and OCS have had the contract ever since.*

offices, it provides services which include office, industrial and window cleaning, laundry, security, hygiene, catering, property maintenance, facilities management and support services.

The Group is also involved in cleaning, laundry, security and hygiene services in Ireland, mainland Europe, North America, South Africa and the Asia Pacific region.

In the United Kingdom, probably the most easily recognised OCS Group company is OCS Cleaning. OCS Cleaning specialises in commercial and industrial markets ranging from site managed contracts to single locations. They pioneered industry training schemes with the British Institute of Cleaning Science for their management and extended NVQ training to cleaning staff around the country. They also have ISO 9002 and are recognised as Investors in People. The culture of the OCS Group encourages every one of its companies to continually innovate and "move with the times". The New Century Cleaning Company is still in business working on high rise buildings high above church

The firm found itself cleaning the Underground Railway Stations, used in the London 'Blitz' as overnight accommodation

spires and factory chimneys. Some work is even carried out by 'abseilers' as skilled as any mountaineer. In order to reduce the cleaning costs of new buildings the firm is frequently called upon to advise architects upon maintenance friendly designs and materials. As modern buildings are often clad in aluminium, stainless steel and powder coated materials in addition to traditional glass, brick and stone new materials and techniques have been developed by New Century.

R Fox & Sons specialise in maintaining and restoring mineral based architectural features in all stones, glass, bronze and other metals.

Smart's Laundry, bought from the retired footballer, has become the OCS Smarts Group Ltd, which provides the ubiquitous washroom services people expect today. Another modern development is the morale boosting provision of clean workwear, known as 'Smartwear' for workers in manufacturing,

Below: *Tom, Gilbert and George, the three Goodliffe Brothers.*

> *Descendants of all three of the Founder's sons and four of his five daughters work or have worked throughout the Group*

retailing and service industries alike. Colours, fit and styles can be chosen in line with corporate image to make a good impression with customers of all types. Dust Control Services exist to protect entrance carpeting by regular changes of dust mats.

Cannon Hygiene is the other OCS company, concentrating in the washroom. Their feminine hygiene service operates all over the country in the commercial and public sector and Cannon Disposables provide all the consumable items such as paper towels and liquid soap.

A nationwide pest control service is provided by Cannon Environmental.

Left: *The Founder and his wife, with their children, at their Norwood home in 1933. Descendants of all three sons and four of the five daughters work or have worked throughout the Group. Left to right back row: Mrs "Queenie" Waud, Mrs "Florrie" Cracknell, Mr Frederick Goodliffe, Mrs Annie Goodliffe, Mr George Goodliffe, Mrs Mabel Spooner. Front row: Mr Gilbert Goodliffe, Mrs Winnie Bowthorpe, Mrs "Eve" Holgate, Mr Tom Goodliffe.*

is now enhanced with use of the most up-to-date electronic CCTV surveillance systems which Centuryan can provide their customers.

Trident Contract Services is OCS Group's specialist, Public Sector market provider. They specialise in providing single and multi-service contracts to hospitals, health care units and schools across the country. These contracts are generally site managed.

Another field of co-operation with local authorities is run by DC Leisure Management which provides management skills for public sports centres.

Dealing with customers' security is the task of Centuryan Security Ltd whose strictly vetted, well trained personnel protect customers' investments to BS7499 standards. The service has a quarter century of experience in providing professional vigilance on all manner of workplaces and development sites. The staff can respond immediately around the clock to dealing with criminal incursions, natural disasters and to offer first aid to those in need. The reduction in the cost of high wastage of goods from factory, goods in transit, and from shops more than covers the employment of Centuryan patrols, low profile 'soft uniform' guards or manned security camera screens. It is a sign of the times that even schools and hospitals are threatened as much as the local water company's offices or a High Street bank. All require modern security. This "modern" security

The qualified sports scientists responsible for instructing the public in leisure pursuits can leave matters such as administration and finance, publicity and legal problems to the experienced professionals of DC Leisure Management.

Select Facilities Services offers businesses a flexible approach to building care so that the customer can concentrate on running their show without spending time on day to day housekeeping tasks. Select can provide staff and can even mastermind the re-location of a client's business to another site, town or country.

OCS provide additional Specialist Services to supplement all its enterprises and to enhance the quality of goods and services provided for

Above: *In the early days, muscle power was the only means of getting a window cleaner's equipment to and from work. An eight mile round trip with a fully loaded truck was not unusual. Right: The Group fleet pictured in the mid 1950s.*

customers. New Century's high travelling window cleaners lives depend on the design and quality of Centuryan Safety Services which makes and installs safety eyebolts and Pushlock devices. Since 1956 Cradle Runways International has led the field in designing, making and installing permanent access equipment on buildings around Britain. TML Ltd offers effective scheduled maintenance but of the mechanical and electrical plant without which modern factories and other buildings could not exist.

The firm of Whitbys was founded over a hundred years ago and, as part of OCS, now provides a 24 hour response to calls, within the M25 Ring Road,

requiring building refurbishment by skilled craftsmen.

Employee morale may be boosted by clean, comfortable working environments and smart clothes but it is positively fed in the canteen or dining room. Sovereign Catering Services operate all around the country in filling the breaks decreed by law when 'the cup that cheers' helps to influence visitors and staff alike for the better. Sovereign is another section of OCS dedicated to easing the management burden of its clients by providing plenty of good food to refresh employee body and mind for the afternoon's work. Any firm with a reputation for a first class product which wants its staff in high fettle to deliver reliable goods or services to their paying customers can rely on Sovereign to provide the impetus.

Everyone enjoys working in, or visiting, a workplace enlivened by living plants. When well looked after foliage plants help clean the air while their shapes and colourful flowers refresh the spirit. Throwers provide and service displays indoors and outside which can soften stark outlines and create a wonderful image. Contracts ensure that small displays receive the same skilled care as do man sized trees and the larger acreages of company sports fields. While plants can lighten the spirit OCS's Lighting Maintenance company can lighten the workplace most effectively. In 1900 gas lit offices and workshops were gloomy with panelling or dirt which eventually led to glaring fluorescent lighting. Science has brought about a greater understanding of the benefits of clear restful lighting in making working conditions pleasant and effective.

Remember the little shipping company at the beginning of the story? Today OCS's Aviation and Airport Services play a vital part in the safe movement of people and goods in the aircraft which have replaced sea going ships. The aviation industry sets rigid codes of security, tight deadlines in aircraft turn around time and spotless grooming of passenger accommodation. The latter includes laundry, water and waste transferral, ferrying services for the disabled and other VIPs and delivery of mislaid luggage. The firm is a member of the IATA and holds ISO 9002EN in recognition of the quality of its work. OCS is truly a child of the Twentieth Century, a hundred years old and ready to show the new Millennium how to get on with the job of providing a range of goods and services contracted by professional staff at every level.

With over 40 trading companies, operating in more than 35 countries and five continents, OCS Group has clearly not rested on its laurels and looks forward to the challenges of the next century. The Guv'nor would have been as proud as Punch!

Above: A mid 1990s photo of the fourth generation of family workers. *Below:* Members of the family working in the business when the Sanderstead offices were opened in 1983.

Technology that rings the changes and changes the rings

In 1935 Stanley Baldwin was Prime Minister, Hitchcock's film The 39 Steps had just been released, and 15-year old Eric Brett got a job at fourpence ha'penny an hour in the Capstan Shop at Radio Instruments Limited, 40 Purley Way, Croydon. Radio Instruments was still quite a new company, having been established there some three years previously, in 1932, by an ex-Admiralty man named Joseph Joseph. The company made a range of radios, from the three-valve Madrigal wireless set to be found in the front parlour of many a home throughout Britain, to the more specialised radio receivers supplied to the Admiralty, the Army, the Air Force, the Post Office and the BBC; and receivers were even exported to Russia. So it was a thriving, forward-looking company which offered good prospects to employees like Eric Brett. The foreman of the Capstan Shop was Jack Clarke, and his assistant was Ernie Anderton; Ernie seems to have been a keen advocate of staff training, as he encouraged Eric to enrol for evening classes to study for his National

Certificates, and Eric took his advice and attended the Croydon Polytechnic in Scarbrook Road on a Sunday evening, to further his education.

Records show that Eric remained with the Company throughout the war years. During this period, under managing director Mr Fearn, output from the Purley Way factory diversified somewhat, becoming rather more specialised to meet the country's military needs with products which included gunsights, rangefinders, theodolites, lenses, cameras and light tools, as well as radio sets. The name of the Company was changed to Aeronautical and General Instruments Limited to reflect the increasing scope of its manufacturing activities. In particular its camera design and manufacture was to become an important facet of the Company's work. AGI cameras were used throughout the war to help gather intelligence information, and indeed their medium and low altitude airborne cameras are still used in aerial photography today to gather high-definition detail of ground installations, and the RAF and the US Navy and Custom Service continue to use the smaller Agiflight 70mm hand-held camera; while AGI's range of small cameras such as the Agiflex and Agifold were the forerunners of today's professional reflex cameras.

At the end of the war the firm became involved in the production of high-class wooden furniture, a temporary diversification which may surprise some readers, but its contribution to technology continued

Top: *Founder Richard Theiler.*
Right: *When the firm partici-pated in a Brussels exhibition it marked the beginning of a period of worldwide expansion from 1910 to 1928.*
Below: *Heinrich Landis, who teamed up with Richard Theiler in 1903 and from whom he took over the business in 1904.*

Above: The company's Croydon site. On the left of the picture is one of Purley Way's famous plane trees (this one, however, was torn down in the 1987 hurricane!).
Below: Karl Heinrich Gyr who joined Heinrich Landis in 1905 to set up the partnership of Landis & Gyr.

with the company establishing itself as the main supplier of the electromagnetic speed and distance log fitted to ships belonging to the majority of the NATO navies, a niche which it was to occupy right up to the 1980s. By this time AGI was well on the way to becoming the world's leading supplier of another piece of technology with which the public will be infinitely more familiar - the payphone. The good business relationship which had existed between the company and the Post Office in the 1930s, when the latter organisation had purchased a large number of Mr Joseph's radio receivers, was renewed during the 1970s, and AGI, under its new managing director Mr John Dearlove, was contracted to supply over a hundred thousand units of the Post Office 700 Series Public Coin Payphone. Since then the company has introduced a succession of new payphone designs to accommodate new telephone technology and new coinages, while a policy of ongoing improvement has resulted in many changes in the manufacturing processes used in the factory at 40 Purley Way since the 1950s. John Dearlove was succeeded as managing director by Hugh Melvin, followed by Terry Clements, David McCormack, Frans Defilet and Martin Brennan. Meanwhile the company's young engineers continued to design and patent the latest electronic coin validation designs. Since the mid-70s the factory has assembled and delivered over 700,000 Agifon payphones, for use both indoors and outdoors, throughout the world.

An important development came about in 1984 when AGI was acquired by the long-established Swiss-based corporation Landis and Gyr. The founder of this company, Richard Theiler, was an outstanding Swiss pioneer in telegraphy and telephony, and both he and his father had received various medals and awards at international exhibitions. Richard's father had settled in London in 1856, working for the Electric Telegraph Company before setting up in business with his sons, making telephone sets. Richard had taken this company over after his father's death in 1873 and continued to run it until 1891, when he sold up and returned to Switzerland. Five years later he had set up his own purpose-built factory in Hofstrasse, Zug, where he manufactured small quantities of electricity meters, to his own patent design, as well as phonograph cylinders, and telephone magnetos for the Swiss Post, Telegraph and Telephone services in Berne. Originally styled 'Electrotechnische Institut Theiler & Co', the firm became H Landis on 30th September 1904 when Heinrich Landis, who had become a partner in 1903 at the age of 24, took the business over from 63-year-old Theiler. The following year the company became Landis & Gyr when Mr Landis in turn entered

Above: An early electricity meters assembly line.

into partnership with Dr Karl Heinrich Gyr. As Landis & Gyr the firm concentrated on the production of electricity meters, and it grew steadily, becoming a limited company in 1914. Mr Landis died in 1922 at the age of 43, having suffered from ill health for many years, and Dr Gyr, a distinguished scientist and a man of great enterprise and energy, proceeded to build the company up into a major international organisation until his own death in 1946. The Group's success in becoming the world's largest maker of electricity meters was attributed to the foresight and hard work of Dr Gyr, and from there it went on to become, by the early 70s, one of Europe's leading manufacturers of a great variety of instruments and systems for metering, measuring, control and regulating functions with a presence world-wide. The takeover of AGI by Landis & Gyr in 1984 therefore represented the coming together of two well-established and respected organisations with a long history of technological expertise in their specialist fields, with the factory at 40 Purley Way becoming the main production facility for the communications division of the Landis & Gyr Corporation. A further recent development in the organisation structure has been the establishment of Landis & Gyr Communications as an independent entity, with Texas Pacific Group as the major shareholder. This will ensure that the company has adequate financial backing, together with the independence to pursue its own manufacturing strategy in the current climate of rapid technological progress, so, by making optimum use of its expertise and experience, it will continue to lead the field.

As soon as the sign over the front porch of 40 Purley Way changed to Landis & Gyr Communications UK Limited to reflect the company's new identity, the range of products made in the factory began to evolve in line with the latest technological advances. One major development was the Optical Card Payphone, supplied to British Telecom; many readers will remember buying their first green phonecard, wondering how it worked but enjoying the prospect of no longer having to load their pockets with coins in advance of making a trunk call from a phone box. A more recent innovation is the Payphone 2000, which will be a familiar sight to travellers passing through Gatwick, Heathrow and Luton airports, and indeed all the major rail and bus stations up and down the country. And in the future all manner of financial transactions will be conducting using Landis & Gyr's range of products which employ the most up-to-date chip card technology. The list of services which can, or soon will, be payed for simply by putting a chip card in a slot includes such everyday activities as parking the car, travelling by public transport or by taxi, and obtaining food and drink from vending machines. Many have already discovered several advantages of using card readers: there is no need to jealously hoard coins of various denominations for future use, and vandals are no longer tempted by the thought of large numbers of coins just waiting to be prised out of a machine. Also, inserting a chip card into a card

reader is much quicker than the traditional system of credit card usage which involves waiting for the transaction slip to be printed, so there is less queuing for the customer; and chip cards are far more secure than the old magnetic stripe cards, so service providers are less vulnerable to fraud. This is an area where there will be many developments in the future - and most of them will no doubt come out of the Purley Way factory. Meanwhile, Landis & Gyr remains the market leader in payphone technology, with over 10 million people a day making phone calls using Landis & Gyr coin and card operated public payphones. The company is committed to using technology in this area to drive down costs, to maintain the highest standards and to satisfy the public's insatiable demand for reliability and novelty with innovative devices and offerings.

Important change in another area has also come about as a result of Landis & Gyr's presence in Purley Way. The introduction of a carefully-planned range of new

Left: *The Blue Payphone - the first electro-magnetic high revenue public coin payphone, introduced into the UK in 1981.*
Below: *Mr and Mrs Tony Blair with Martin Brennan during their visit to Landis & Gyr in 1997.*

Above: *A selection of payphones produced by Landis & Gyr.* ***Right:*** *The Prime Minister and his wife Cherie Blair during their visit.*

systems and procedures reflects the Group's policy of improving both its ecological and its economic efficiency - termed its eco-efficiency. Since setting up a Corporate Environmental Office in 1992, the organisation has steadily increased its environmental activities, and in 1995 an extensive study of the historic contamination of the 64 year old Purley Way site was carried out by a team of environmental specialists. The results of this study have been used in planning an ongoing programme of improvements; among the first steps taken were the implementation of a comprehensive recycling strategy and the elimination of CFCs on the site, and each year a set of environmental objectives and targets are agreed, with the aim of improving the quality of its goods and the health of the environment through the overall efficiency of the company. Progress is monitored, and an annual report detailing the company's 'eco-performance' over the year is made available to the public. This serious commitment to green issues will remain an important part of the company's development policy in the years to come.

With its leading-edge manufacturing techniques and its high quality systems, Landis & Gyr has an important role to play in the education of the next generation of employees. Youngsters who visit the

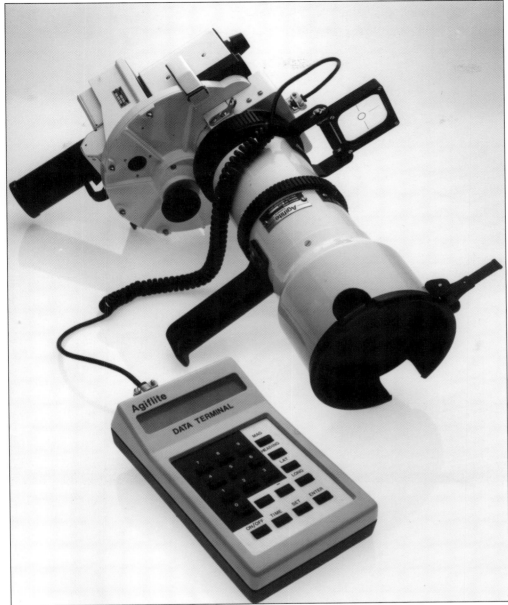

around the world. Closer to home, the many thousands of Croydon-based women and men who have worked in the factory at 40 Purley Way over almost 70 years have enjoyed secure and worthwhile employment, and have shared in the many activities which the company has organised to bring employees and their families together socially. And one splendid local event sponsored by Landis & Gyr which will still be fresh in the minds of most readers was the magnificent Tudor Pageant, held on 23rd March 1996. This event was staged to commemorate the 400th anniversary of the Whitgift Foundation, which fortuitously coincided with the centenary of Landis & Gyr. The pageant was a celebration of the life of Archbishop John Whitgift, and launched a whole week of events with a Tudor theme. Hundreds of residents in period costumes took part, and besides

factory are frequently amazed by how clean and tidy the Purley Way factory is; reactions from a group of A-level design technology students from John Fisher School who visited the factory in the first half of 1999 included such comments as, 'I expected oily stuff everywhere but it's well organised, bright and a good working environment,' 'I'm actually thoroughly amazed,' and 'This would be a wonderful company to work for'.

The young lady who made the latter observation perhaps spoke more truly than she knew. On her brief visit she had seen enough to evaluate the excellence of the working conditions, the smooth running of the organisation and the efficiency of the company's management techniques. However, a quick tour of the factory gives scant opportunity to appreciate the company's long tradition of service to the community, at various levels. On a world-wide scale, first Radio Instruments, then AGI and now Landis & Gyr have played an important part in the development of products which have made a major contribution to the well-being of their fellow citizens

providing people with a great deal of fun and happy memories the extravaganza raised a lot of money for the Mayday Heartbeat appeal to re-equip the cardiology unit at Mayday University Hospital, Thornton Heath.

Young Eric Brett, the lad who started work at 40 Purley Way in 1935 for fourpence ha'penny an hour, might not recognise the factory's products today. But he would recognise the company's commitment to the principle of making a product to provide a service, and he would recognise, too, the high manufacturing standards from which the firm has never deviated. An article published in the Croydon Times during the 1930s said that 'scrupulous care, highly skilled workmanship, and constant experiment are the hallmark of all their products.' Seventy years later, this statement is as true as ever.

Above: *Agiflite - the 70mm hand held airborne military reconnaissance camera in service with the Royal Airforce and the US Customs Service.*

At home or abroad, a company that deals in dignity

The death of a loved one is a bitter blow whenever and wherever it falls. However expected, it is still a sadness that we all are touched with at various stages of our lives. At a time when the world as you know it has been torn apart, there is a need for sympathy. That comes in large amounts from those around us. It is with the more basic requirements that follow a bereavement that the emotional problems start. There are forms to fill in, solicitors to contact, ministers with whom to liaise and authorities to be notified. It is then that the tears often come when unthinking, if not uncaring people, put their foot in it. A careless word here, or an offhand remark there, and the floodgates can open. The last person you want to be unsympathetic is the funeral director. There are practical considerations to be discussed. There is no way of avoiding the talk of coffins, burial, cremation and hearses. However, it is how this is done that counts. A firm such as Rowland Brothers has 125 years of experience on which to draw. Death with dignity is the way the business has been conducted all those years. Without such an approach, there would have been no business. A professional and caring attitude is also commented on,

remembered and spoken about to others. Such is the way that the reputation of the Rowland Brothers grew.

It was in the good old days of Queen Victoria that the family funeral business began. When you hear of Victorian values, it is as well to remember that they included overcrowding, disease and a high mortality rate. As well as prosperity for some, the Industrial Revolution brought large numbers of folk into the towns and cities. Living in cramped conditions, they fell prey to the poor sanitation and health care of the times. Those were not quite the good old days people try to suggest. In such a climate, the role of the funeral services was a busy one. William H Rowland started the business in 1875. Originally, it was combined with the building trade. In the early days, William was more concerned with the painting, decorating and property aspects than with the undertaking.

However this side of the firm disappeared after the Great War of 1914-18. Staff were hard to come by, as King and country made demands on the services

Above: *An early invoice.* ***Below:*** *Harry Rowland conducting the last horse drawn funeral service in 1933, Uncle Jim is on the right hand side of the hearse.*

of young men but the funeral business went from strength to strength. By the end of the 20th century it had seen two world wars, several economic crises and hyperinflation. Despite these and other trials and tribulations that came its way, the firm has now developed into an international concern. It is as ready to deal with bereavements on the other side of the world as it is with those in its own back yard. The headquarters on Whitehorse Road have been the base for five generations of the Rowland family. Now, the premises include several houses that have been a mixture of living accommodation and office space. There are large workshops manufacturing coffins and stonework for monuments and memorials. A garage complex holds the

fleet of hearses and limousines. There are also closed hearses and other vehicles used in the overseas business, carrying loved ones to or from aircraft on that final journey across the water. A chapel of remembrance, where the bereaved can spend a quiet moment in peace and tranquillity with the departed, was erected in 1953. A new chapel complex was built in 1985 catering for all religions including, Church of England, Roman Catholic, Greek Orthodox, Hindu, Sikh and Salvation Army viewing chapels.

It is all a far cry from the horse drawn hearse with its shiny handles and ornate brasses, that used to trundle the streets of Croydon. The funeral director and his staff would have looked both smart and sombre in their long overcoats and velvet trimmed top hats. Walking alongside the carriage, their presence helped the relatives gain strength from the calm way they went about their business. A custom that continued for many decades showed how people gave respect to the occasion. Complete strangers would stop and remove their caps as the funeral procession went by. Even motor cars would slow and let the cortege proceed on its measured way. Those little signs of bygone values seem to have been lost in the hustle, bustle and hurly-burly of the modern world. They were the values that William Rowland instilled in his four sons. By 1932, only one of them, Harry, had survived. It was in 1933 that the last of the regular horse drawn funerals took place. Harry continued to run the business, until the offices were damaged by a bomb in 1943. Arthur's wife Muriel then ran the company from the patched up offices until 1945. Harry's two sons, Arthur and James were fighting in deserts of North Africa and in the Normandy landings respectively. On their return they had to rebuild the business. The Luftwaffe had destroyed so much in their blitz on London and the Home Counties. Rowland's did not escape unscathed. At the end of the second world war, the premises were little more than a shed and some outbuildings. Tools had disappeared and timbers lay rotting, amidst the rubble of the other buildings. There was nothing else for it but to rebuild. This they did and the business rose again from the rubble. Arthur's sons, Tony,

Above: *A Sea Cadets funeral in the late 1950s.*
Left: *The Head Office pictured in 1959.*

a Rowland's agent in nearly every town or seaside resort across Europe and in every major city in the world. Distance is no object. Contacts in far away countries ensure an efficient and caring service. The company has even had dealings in Russia and China. It takes a lot of experience and know-how to be able to work with the regulations and practices that exist in other countries. The pitfalls are tremendous. As well as dealing with grieving relatives who, in some cases, are separated from their loved ones, there is the bureaucracy to go through. There are forms to be filled in correctly, Customs people to be negotiated with and delayed or diverted aircraft to be tracked. One of the more tricky areas is when dealing

David and Bob, later took over and, with sister Jacki, continued to expand the humble funeral director into a prominent family funeral directors in the Croydon area. They were joined by Tony's wife, Margaret and David's wife, Janet. Melanie and Stephen, Tony's children, are members of the latest generation of the family to have played an active role. They joined in 1983 and 1990, respectively. David's son, Andrew also joined the business in 1997 to form a true family concern.

In 1971 Tony developed the company into Rowland Brothers International whose influence now reaches across the globe with its repatriation service. It seems that there is

with the customs and practices of another faith or culture. It is so easy to offend without meaning to. Rowland's staff have been well trained to respect the beliefs of others. As the company has become an international concern since the 1970s, ethnic minorities have come to rely on the sympatetic service provided at home and abroad. For example, for Muslim funerals there is a special washing room, with white tiled walls and a marble floor. There are special coffin covers and unbleached cloth kept in stock.

Above: *A Rolls Royce Hearse, 1965.*
Top: *A local stall holder's funeral going through a Surrey street market.*

Through their international contacts, the firm has the quality caskets, coffins and urns from around the world that place them at the forefront of the funeral directing industry. There is African mahogany, English and Japanese oak, as well as elm wood and fine hand crafted Italian coffins.

Bob Rowland has been developing the monumental masons division and has won several contracts including restoring several war memorials in the Croydon area and the memorial of the founder of the FA Cup. Bob has also developed a new service to the funeral directing, that of grave maintenance plans.

Rowland Brothers provides more than just a funeral service. It provides a pre-paid plan to meet funeral expenses. It was one of the first companies in the UK to do this. In 1984 Tony Rowland developed Golden Leaves pre-paid funeral plans. Since then Golden Leaves has been further developed by Tony's son Stephen into a company providing funeral plans throughout the UK, Spain and Portugal and maybe at some the point the rest of the world.

Relatives are treated with respect and consideration. Most funeral directors would tell you they do the same. But, this company goes much further. It does not just talk of caring after the ceremony and beyond and into the community, it actually does something about it. Occasional lectures and workshops are given. Counselling can be arranged and special advice given on coping with loss. The skill of making sense of death when explaining to a child is a particularly difficult art on which Rowland's can advise. When the Purley branch was opened in 1995, a special fortnight was arranged when local community carers were given the chance to speak to the public. Delicate matters, like cot death and social security benefits to help with expenses, were included. The subjects did not confine themselves to bereavement. There was also guidance from Age Concern, the Terence Higgins Trust and investment groups. In this and other ways, the after care service is one of the important features of the Rowland's service.

The family's wishes are of the greatest importance. A simple or a specialised funeral such as a horse drawn hearse re-introduced in Croydon by Rowland Brothers 50 years later in the 1980s can be arranged. Rowland's make it their aim to provide the same professinoal and caring attention required by all families.

Above: *Three generations of the Rowland family and pictured in 1994.* **Below:** *Tony in the centre with brothers David and Bob at Heathrow Airport with the elements of transport utilised by Rowland Brothers International.*

Looking to the past for the transport of the future

Why throw the baby out with the bathwater? When Britain's road transport system was overhauled in the middle years of the 20th century, the way forward for travel in and around our major towns and cities seemed to be by using more and more double decker buses and private cars. The flirtation with the trolley bus came and went, but the biggest loser was the tram. The tramlines, snaking their way across our streets, were once a major feature for the shopper and worker getting into and out of the town centre. They provided a reliable and cheap method of public transport, dating back to the Victorian age. The first ones were horse drawn, but, with the widespread use of that newfangled discovery, electricity, the sparks from the pantograph, connecting the tramcar to the overhead cables, were soon changing the face of our cities. As well as being efficient, they were the joy of the youngster in giving him tickets to collect and memories to keep. They even inspired Americans into song. 'Clang, clang, clang went the trolley'; it being their word for our tram. Yet, it was felt that they slowed traffic on the streets to a crawl. The motor bus was more flexible in the path it followed. The motor car was more nippy. By the 1950s, there were few companies operating the tram any more and it was destined to become a museum piece, something to show children what great-grandma used to ride on. However, by the 1980s, the huge number of cars

Above: An early tram in North End, Croydon.
Below: Trams at the Tramlink Depot.

clogging the roads and the pollution they caused was making councils and government rethink its strategy. Privatised minibuses now ran where those '97 horse-power omnibuses', that Michael Flanders sang about, used to go. Cars were prohibited in some town centres and tolls were being charged to enter others. Guess what was decided? It would be a good idea to reintroduce the tram.

London Transport and British Rail joined forces in 1986 to publish the result of a joint survey on the capital city's transport needs. The whole of Greater London was put under the microscope and the seeds of Tramlink were sown. From 1990, London Transport and Croydon Council have been working as a joint operation in promoting the scheme. As long ago as 1991, the local population was asked its opinion about which routes would be needed and best subscribed. The majority was in favour of the venture. The hours spent in traffic jams, queuing to get into car parks and the seemingly endless lines of traffic leaving the city in the evening rush hour were problems which had to be solved. It was in

November 1993 that the Croydon Tramlink Bill came before Parliament. With some minor amendments by the Select Committees, the Bill received the Royal assent in July 1994 and so London Regional transport was given the approval to build and run Tramlink and together with the London Borough of Croydon developed specifications for performance. In late 1995 these were put out to tender.

Companies and consortia had to be attracted to finance and design the whole operation, as well as build and run it. Tramtrack Croydon Ltd was formed to carry out this work. Included in the

Left: *Tram with Purley Way retail area in view.*
Below: *Passengers boarding a tram at the Therapia Lane tram stop.*

group were the operators, First CentreWest, the tram suppliers, Bombardier Transportation and McAlpine/Amey Construction, which provided the civil engineering expertise in track laying, bridge building and electrical systems. The Royal Bank of Scotland and 3i provided financial support. Some of the money came from central Government coffers and the rest from Tramtrack Croydon Ltd. This is only right as the benefit will be felt by other road users with traffic congestion reduced and travel time slashed. Work began in earnest in 1997 and it was intended to have the first tram easing through the streets of Croydon before the end of 1999.

All these preparations have to be carried out with a thought for our wider future. In the past, our ancestors did what they liked for the 'now' of the occasion. In modern times we have to think of the 'tomorrow'. Our planet is becoming so overcrowded with people and

This picture: *A tram passing the familiar towers at Ikea, Purley Way Retail Area.*

pollution that we can no longer live like ostriches. We have to lift our heads and look at the effects our actions might have on those who follow us. Tramlink will give a public service that is efficient in its energy consumption and in the way that fuel is used. Electricity is a clean energy and the tramcars will be able to carry 50 motor car loads of people on a 30 metre tram that is the same length as just six cars. As a full tram can carry over 200 people and cars often only have one occupant, the comparative figure is probably even more impressive. Just imagine; no fumes and no need for road widening. A dual carriageway road takes up three times as much space as a double tramtrack. Also to be considered are the discomfort and dangers of an exhaust pouring out diesel fumes into your face, whilst seated at the wheel of the car behind, waiting for the lights to change. Any reduction in the 880,000 tonnes of carbon dioxide, that finds a way into the skies above Croydon each year, must be an improvement. Many miles of converted Railtrack lines have been used, so reducing the need to lay every yard anew. Where fresh track has been laid, it has helped to speed up transport. Trams can pull up hills and get round tight bends that conventional trains cannot manage.

It is good to see that the making of a profit can be done hand in hand with consideration for the environment. The damage to trees has been kept to a minimum. Replanting and landscaping has been part of the brief and thought has even been given to the type of soil brought into the area, so that it remains sympathetic with that found naturally in the Addington Hills. In that way, the life of plants and the world of the small creatures that rely on them, can continue largely unchanged. Badgers have received special attention as work progressed. They were given tunnels under the tracks, safety fences and runs to guide them from the sett to the tunnel where they would normally cross the line. Brock has been well served. Open spaces for the public have been cleared or created at Stroud Green well

and Threehalfpenny Wood. So, the two footed animals have their little runs and tunnels, too.

The good thing about this tram service is that it is part of an integrated transport system. Instead of trying to compete with other ways of getting from A to Z, it is seeing how each link of the transport chain can be clipped together. The mainline rail stations at Wimbledon, Mitcham, East and West Croydon, Elmers End and Beckenham all have direct connections with Tramlink. Also at Wimbledon is the link up with the Underground. Bus services will inter-connect with Tramlink at a large number of bus stops. The new bus interchange at Addington gives access to the feeder routes around Biggin Hill and Forestdale. The safety and convenience factors have been given high priority. Tracks are flush with the road surface, so that pedestrians can cross safely and easily. Platforms have been adjusted, so that boarding can take place without the need to step up or down. This is a boon for shoppers with heavy bags, mums with twins in the buggy and the elderly or infirm. The 24 trams have 38 stopping places that are well lit at night and covered by CCTV. Shelters with seating, displayed timetables, automatic ticket machines and a clear information display system all help improve the service.

As time goes by, the success of Tramlink will be measured as much by the number of cars it takes off the road as by the number of passengers it carries. Sheffield and Manchester were positive about the early days of their versions of Tramlink and, perhaps, the best recommendation came from one disabled passenger in the French city of Grenoble. When trams were reintroduced, she said, 'They have given me back my city'.

Below: *A tram passing the Whitgift Hospital on its journey from George Street to Crown Hill.*

The company that has been 'expanding' for more than 60 years

A familiar landmark on the Croydon industrial scene since before the war has been the highly successful and unique foam manufacturing business that now operates as Zotefoams plc. It has a long tradition of innovation and a remarkable pedigree that links it with some of the greatest names in plastics history.

It was in the mid-30s that the move from its Wembley site to Mitcham Road was completed. The Bakelite Company had been formed ten years previously from the amalgamation of the British Xylonite Company and the Damard Lacquer Company, and in fact its roots can be traced as far back as 1877. During the early 30s it had been involved in the production of decorative laminates known as Warerite, which were extensively used in fitting out two liners, the Queen Mary and the Queen Elizabeth. The company began producing Rubazote expanded rubber in 1935, but development of the market was slow. Ownership of the company subsequently passed to St Helen's Cable & Rubber Company, after which the business changed hands several more times. Following flotation on the stockmarket three years later, the company was established in the form in which we know it today -

Zotefoams plc, a leading name in the highly competitive world of polyolefin foam manufacturing.

A series of interesting developments, exciting discoveries and innovative products highlights the company's progress from the Rubazote® of the 1930s to the wide range of foams produced today. Rubazote itself owed much to the work of Birmingham-born scientist Charles Lancaster Marshall, who

Left: *Fritz Pfleumer holding a section of expanded rubber material used for tyre filling in 1910.*
Bottom: *Charles Lancaster Marshall, founder of Onazote Limited in 1921.* **Below:** *The Palace of Arts of the British Empire Exhibition at Wembley was purchased by the Expanded Rubber Co. Ltd in 1927.*

was interested in experiments performed in Austria with various types of expanded materials, including expanded rubbers, to make a 'puncture-proof' tyre. Marshall eventually developed and patented his own process for making expanded rubbers of all kinds and set up a company called Onazote Limited, a name derived from the French 'azote', meaning nitrogen. Onazote® was also the name of one of its products, an expanded ebonite (ebonite is hard, as opposed to soft, rubber).

Production of Rubazote at Croydon was to continue right up until 1974, although it was interrupted during the second world war when, after the fall of Singapore, natural rubber became very scarce. Various innovations in the use of rubber were developed to meet wartime needs. Onazote found a number of military applications, from the cockpits of midget submarines to the nose of the 'Valiant' bomber. The company also developed new processes for making special soft rubber which could be used for self-sealing tanks for aircraft. Its products were in such demand that two additional factories were opened, one in Slough and one in Dundee; output included buoyancy materials for boom defences, insulation materials for special containers and trailing cable for combating magnetic mines. Other products developed during this period included an expanded vinyl, Formvar, which had great impact strength, and the company also worked with urea-formaldehyde resins, expanding these into a material called FUF, which looked like snow and was used to create the blizzard effects in the famous film 'Scott of the Antarctic.'

Innovation continued in the mid-50s with the introduction of Polyzote®, an expanded polystyrene, which remained a popular product throughout the 60s.

This digression into work with plastics was to have far-reaching consequences as it was without doubt one of the factors

Top left: Henry Neal Shelmerdine who was put in charge of the company in 1938. **Above:** Loading 'FUF' (urea formaldehyde foam) for use as snow in the film 'Scott of the Antarctic'. **Below:** An early view of the Croydon premises.

which led to the acquisition of a controlling interest by BX Plastics, which in turn led to its transfer to the parent company BXL. However, in the post-war years, rubber became once again central to the company's activities, with its two most important products being Rubazote and Onazote. During this period, it was also making a sponge rubber branded Zote®, microcellular shoe soling materials, and an imaginative product named Rubacurl which was in fact rubberised hair.

Then, in 1962 Plastazote® was launched. This remarkable material, based on the plastics polyethylene ('polythene'), has found a wide range of specialised applications in fields as diverse as automotive and civil engineering, marine buoyancy, electronics, commercial packaging and general industry, and particularly in healthcare,

where, because it can be moulded around the patient's body, it is ideal for splinting applications. Hospitals throughout the world use Plastazote to make devices such as neck and body splints, special footwear and devices to support damaged or deformed limbs. Plastazote, together with Evazote® (which was launched in 1968 and is a similar material to Plastazote, but is more rubber-like and resilient) were the product range at this time.

The Croydon factory has not used rubber as raw material since 1974. Trading conditions in the rubber market had been difficult for some while, and at the same time the company was becoming increasingly interested in exploiting the potential of using the same manufacturing techniques on more sophisticated and specialised materials. When Rubazote was finally discontinued, it had been in production

for almost 40 years, and during that time it had found hundreds of applications. Perhaps the single application which will ensure Rubazote is never forgotten is the role it played in the classic film 'Moby Dick', where Gregory Peck's co-star the Great White Whale was made out of an ultralight-density sheet of Rubazote spread over a wooden frame and covered with latex. The mid-70s also saw the sale of the expanded polystyrene business.

The late 1980s and 1990s have seen the development of an exciting range of applications for Zotefoams' technologically-advanced products, opening up into a range of exciting and attractive possibilities. It has also been an era of expansion: in 1989 the company established a strong presence on the Continent through its purchase of a foam company at Alcala de Henares in Spain. It also acquired the X-Cell factory in Dundee, thus renewing its connections with a city where the company had previously had a factory in the later years of the war. In 1992 the company was first rebadged to BP

Above left: *Zotefoam in 1950.* **Top:** *A tanker insulated with Plastazote.*

Chemicals' corporate standards and it was then subject of the management buy-out which established Zotefoams Limited. Following flotation on the stockmarket three years later, the company was established in the form in which we know it today - Zotefoams plc. International growth has continued: a subsidiary, Zotefoams Inc, has been established in the North American market to cope with rapidly growing demand for the Zotefoams range of products in the USA, and production is scheduled to commence at the beginning of the next millennium.

Throughout the history of this remarkable company, being affiliated at various stages in its life to the British Xylonite Company Limited, Distillers, Union Carbide Corporation, and finally BP Chemicals, three factors have played an important part: the process, the product and the management. Of the three, the process is the one which has remained constant. It is the unique two-stage gassing process, high pressure nitrogen impregnation and low pressure expansion, that has enabled the company to develop the innovative products - all of them totally environmentally friendly - which over the years have been so beneficial to so many aspects of our lives. From the original expanded rubber foams to the new light cross-linked foams and metallocene-catalysed grades, each product has found niches to fill and made itself invaluable both in everyday use and in specialised applications. In 1981 Plastazote was singled out for especial recognition when the Duke of Edinburgh presented the company with a gold medal in recognition of the contribution made by Plastazote foam in the Service of Mankind.

Zotefoams plc is totally committed to the continuing development, production and international marketing of these unique products, and the Croydon workforce, which since 1936 has taken great pride in the goods it has produced, looks forward to taking its world-beating products into the next millennium.

Today, Zotefoams plc makes closed cell foams. Specifically, it makes a range of foams described technically as nitrogen-blown polyolefin materials, and more specifically still it is the only manufacturer in the world to make these products. Its range of technologically advanced products such as Plastazote, Evazote, Supazote®, and Propozote® (Supazote is a supersoft foam and Propozote is a polypropylene foam), each with a worldwide range of specialised applications, is manufactured using a unique process - a process which is exclusive to Croydon, and, furthermore, one which has been in use at Croydon since 1936.

Left: *Jensen specified Plastazote for its impact/energy absorption properties for their cars.*
Below: *An aerial view of the Croydon premises.*

Pep up your life

All this talk of PEPs and ISAs is confusing enough without having to move into the world of securities, capital gains tax and pensions. Left on your own you will struggle through the vast amount of literature in the financial press and come out as confused as when you began. Then there is the junk mail that seems to make up half of the stuff dropping through our letter boxes these days. Pity the poor postman struggling up the road with another sack full of offers to make us rich with index trackers and unit trusts. Since a lot of what he delivers ends up in the bin, he must get really frustrated knowing that, as fast as he puts it on the doormat, it disappears along with the potato peelings. The reason is that a lot of people now have the common sense not to try to plough their own furrow in such a complicated field. The role of the independent financial advisor is with us. Since the

> *The office equipment was one desk two chairs and a portable typewriter*

pension scandals of recent years, their work has become even more important in guiding the general public in the best way of investing for the future that is also best for them and not just best for the salesman or insurance company. Every advisor worth his salt is a member of the well regulated Personal Investment Authority. Under the watchful eye of the PIA, financial services are offered without bias and for the benefit of the individual customer. This is important. Each person has his own particular needs and a package or portfolio needs to be tailored just for him or her.

Such a company group, Francis Townsend and Hayward, is based

Below: Harry Flower Snr (left), War Correspondent for the Daily Telegraph with German Airmen captured near Tenterten in Kent during the Battle of Britain.

on South End. It has been here since about 1960, though it only occupied the ground floor shop frontage area in those days. Life for the firm had begun the year before in a tiny room on High Street, in a building owned by the estate agents, Arnott and Bear. It was many a mile from the computerised office of to-day. The world of Micropal and internet banking were light years away. The office equipment was one desk, two chairs and a portable typewriter. The value of all that would not buy you a one year subscription and calls to a mobile phone at to-day's prices. But, as Mao Tse Tung put it, a march of 1,000 miles begins with but a single step. It was a time of great optimism in the country. Employment was high and the order books of businesses were full. The prime minister of the day, Harold Macmillan, had told everybody in the land that they had never 'had it so good'. He was right. We had money in our pockets to spend and invest. This was where the founders of Francis Townsend & Company, as it was originally called, came in. Ron Quinton, a magistrate in nearby Wallington, and Harry Flower were inspectors working for the Norwich Union. They were well schooled in the financial sector. Part of their jobs had seen them involved in visiting agents and bank managers to persuade them to use the services and products that the Norwich Union provided. It was a large step to go it alone, but they went for it and took the plunge.

Above: *An aerial view of Croydon, dating from 1936.* **Left:** *Kevin Hains and Douglas Flower.*

At first, with only secretarial staff as back up, it was a struggle to keep their heads above water. If Macmillan had walked past, he would have been reminded of his message of hope in no uncertain manner! For the first six months, both partners lived on their savings. They drew no income and ploughed everything back into the business. Even the cars they bought were ex-company vehicles from their former employers. However, big business does sometimes have a heart. The cars were sold to the partners at a favourable rate. The business merged with William Bell & Company, a firm that had been set up in 1947, and the light at the end of the tunnel started to shine a little more brightly. Concentrating on life insurance and general policies for mortgages, car, home and retirement, Mr Flower and Mr Quinton felt able to move to the more comfortable premises on South End. Other family members supported them, giving valuable help in establishing the business as a fledgling that was to grow into one of Croydon's most respected insurance broker and financial services provider. Mrs G Quinton was the secretary and Harry Flower Senior distributed sales and product literature. He had retired from his journalistic work with the Daily Telegraph, for whom he had been a war correspondent. He could now lend a hand in a new battle zone, that of the financial sector. Ron Quinton concentrated on the life business and his partner on the general insurance side in those earlier days. A family connection into a third generation has been established. Douglas Flower joined in 1990. He had been a director in a similar company before joining his father. Before that, he had worked for Norwich Union, so completing the cycle as the founders of Francis Townsend

Top: *Lunch with Anita Dobson celebrating Harry Flower's runner-up award of IFA of the Year.*
Above right: *Ron Quinton and Harry Flower.*

and Hayward had done before. Mr Quinton ceased to be a director as the 1980s drew to a close, but he continued to be involved for the best part of another 10 years. His co-founder retired towards the end of the 1990s.

In 1999, the company celebrated its 40th anniversary. It had a ruby background as well as a rosy future. But, how things have changed in the market place in that time. There are now some 20 people on the staff and the business has grown at such a degree that it has split into separate companies. The Insurance Broking Company arranges policies with over 50 companies and with Lloyds. Household policies, contents, buildings etc and motor insurance cover still provide a solid amount of business. Commercial insurance has expanded as large companies and small businesses seek cover for their trading risks. It is here where the vast experience of the staff scores. Together, there are hundreds of years of know how to be tapped. Allied to the experience are the qualifications that people have gained through the studying of the world of finance, administration and brokerage. The current chairman, Fred Bleasdale, is a former president of the Association of Chartered Certified Accountants, the Treasurer of Esso and an assistant general manager of the Midland Bank. The company has been able to combine this expertise and experience with its strong local connections. There is a special link with local sport. Harry Flower spent 29 seasons battling through the mud and the scrums of the rugby field. If he had any edge to him, that was knocked off long ago! The cut and thrust of the business world was easy meat for someone used to taking on a lock forward hammering at

him. He became president of Old Purlians Rugby Club and son, Douglas, has been involved with the club since 1979. They breed them loyal in the Flower family. Partly through these connections, a lot of business is conducted with sports clubs - rugby, hockey, golf and cricket, in particular

The Financial Services Company grew out of necessity and public demand. Mortgages and life insurance is still arranged, but a lot of the work is taken up with all manner of investment. Retirement and pensions, taxation and growth are subjects that occupy much of the work. The people at Francis Townsend and Hayward sleep easy in their beds, knowing that sound, reliable, unbiased advice has been given to their clients. They will range from high profile folk in the acting profession and other celebrities to public limited companies and to humble you and I. No matter how important the customer, each one is of equal worth to the staff in this firm. With this sort of attitude in providing an efficient and bespoke service, it came as no surprise that Harry Flower was the runner up in the national awards for the Best Corporate Independent Financial Advisor of 1993. The managing director, Kevin Hains, was shortlisted for the same award in 1998.

As the company looks to expand the retirement planning and investment business by launching a new company to deal with this side, it continues to build on the commercial side, meeting the various medical, property and liability cover it needs. In the past, several people helped by the company became millionaires. It has even insured Albert Hall, though let's be truthful. That was the name of a chap working in a department store!

Left: *Fred Bleasdale, Chairman since 1994.*
Below: *The FTH Insurance Broking Team.*

A poppet in a factory in a Surrey orchard

Sitting on the back row of the cinema, with a poppet in one hand and a poppet by your side. How many love affairs and marriages began in this way? The poppet by your side was the love of your life, but it was made all the sweeter by that box of chocolate coated raisins, toffees or creams that were Paynes Poppets. How many films or plays have these tasty delights appeared at? Add in the 'Just' range, like Just Brazils, Just Ginger and Just Mints and you have an exotic range of tastes and treasures to tempt even the most jaded palate. All kinds of different centres, both man-made and natural, have been coated with any of three different chocolate covers over a period of more than 60 years.

It was when the docks of East London were flourishing in the late Victorian era that George Payne began his business in 1896. As a blender and packager of tea and coffee, the company quickly expanded. By Edwardian times, there were premises in Glasgow, Leeds, Manchester and Liverpool. Abroad, there were outlets in South Africa, India and Ceylon (Sri Lanka). By the 1990s, this side of the business was with Finlay Beverages and based in Swindon and South Elmsall, in Yorkshire. However, a new drink, Lift Instant Lemon Tea, stayed with Paynes. It is estimated that over a million cups of this refreshing and unique brew are now supped annually.

In 1905, the company started cocoa production in SE London. It was only natural that this should develop into the side of the business that has brought so many people together and made Paynes a household name. By 1910, chocolate making had begun in factories on Queen Elizabeth Street, in London, and Three Oak Lane.

Top left: *George Payne, founder of the company.* **Top right:** *The firm's original premises at Tower Bridge.* **Left:** *Some of the company's earlier products.*

It was just after World War I that the company came to Croydon. The site was bought in 1919 and opened as a factory two years later. Situated on the Beddington Place Estate, this was the 'Factory in a Surrey orchard'. Paynes was one of the first of the forward thinking companies that valued its workers and the local community. Close to the factory was an eight acre recreation field. Soccer, cricket and tennis facilities were provided and enjoyed by the firm's employees and their families. It helped to form a strong bond between the man or woman on the shop floor and the managers and directors who worked 'above' them. The warm, strong smell of the cocoa bean hung around as they were graded and sorted. The large batteries of roasters, heated by coke and steam. broke the beans into small pieces of cocoa 'nibs'. From here they were milled into powder. After sugar and cocoa butter were added, the mix would be rolled into the smooth, rich paste that would become Paynes Chocolates.

After the death of the founder, in 1927, Henry Payne took over the reins of the business. It was under his chairmanship that in 1937 the dragee based confectionery product was developed. This was the birth of the Poppet. However, the mass appeal of Poppets took the name of Paynes to a much wider clientele. The quality was not sacrificed, but the new market of fast moving consumer goods brought a different era for Paynes. Running side by side with the more upmarket brazils, pineapple fourrees and vintage liqueur chocolates, the confectionery side of the business was now a household name in both manor house and humble terrace. Although damaged in various air raids in the blitz of 1940 and 1941, production continued through those difficult years. Materials were in short supply and transport hard to arrange, but the company soldiered on. Henry Payne died in 1946, but the seeds of further expansion had been sown. In June 1999, the Confectionery and Lift Tea Division were bought out by Northern Foods, but the name of Paynes trades on. Cocoa from Africa, nuts from Bolivia, raisins from California and ginger from Australia continue to be imported and turned into a chocolate or confectionery that is something extra special.

Above: *A well-known advertisement for probably the company's most famous product.*
Below: *An aerial view of the modern premises.*

Insuring a bright future

We all need insurance in case the worst happens. It seems to be an ever increasing drain on our purses. There is the car to cover, the house to insure and the contents to be taken care of. When the holidays come, we will need travel, sickness and property insurance. There is also assurance against the inevitable in the form of life cover. That is only a start. What about cover for special events? Policies in case we have twins, the wedding day is rained off, the builder falls off our roof and the cat needs to be operated on. Private health insurance, with profits policies, endowments etc; where does it all end? But imagine the opposite scenario - no insurance. The house burns down, the electrical goods and jewellery are stolen, the car goes for a joyride, the plumbing in the holiday hotel gives us all typhoid...Stop! We are convinced. Insurance is a necessity. But, that is only the beginning of the problem. Where to go to for the best deal or advice? Surprisingly, many contact an insurance company direct. It is hardly surprising that they recommend their own products. A better idea is to get in touch with a broker who can find the

right match for you or tailor make a policy that is best suited. HR Jennings & Company Ltd have been doing just that since 1922. Founded by Henry Rowland Jennings, the insurance broking and estate management of those days was carried out in London EC2, on Gresham Street. It moved to Milk Street after the second world war, staying until 1971 when the business was bought by FS Haigh. He had been established in Croydon as an insurance broker, controlling a small group of companies. Offices for the business were now established on Wellesley Road.

Henry Jennings' son, Robert Rowland Jennings, inherited the firm on his father's death in 1933. He had previously worked as a director in the company. He piloted Jennings & Co through the difficult war years, when business could do little more than be kept ticking over. He died in 1969. Everything was hand-written into big ledgers.

Above: '*Car & General' logo - circa 1955 (before takeover by Royal Exchange).* ***Below:*** *Croydon Airport and Aerodrome Hotel - circa 1932.*

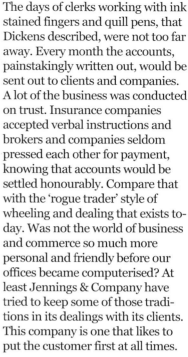

The days of clerks working with ink stained fingers and quill pens, that Dickens described, were not too far away. Every month the accounts, painstakingly written out, would be sent out to clients and companies. A lot of the business was conducted on trust. Insurance companies accepted verbal instructions and brokers and companies seldom pressed each other for payment, knowing that accounts would be settled honourably. Compare that with the 'rogue trader' style of wheeling and dealing that exists to-day. Was not the world of business and commerce so much more personal and friendly before our offices became computerised? At least Jennings & Company have tried to keep some of those traditions in its dealings with its clients. This company is one that likes to put the customer first at all times.

Jennings & Company is now based at Aviation House on Brighton Road. The name comes from its connection with the aircraft business. Between 1972 and 1983, the company occupied the control tower at the Croydon Airport Terminal Building. The airport had closed in 1959, so there was no danger of the draught of low flying planes blowing policies off the table! Croydon Airport had been the world's largest airport in its heyday of 1928. Norman Pocock, the present managing director, had joined the firm in 1961. He had a history in car insurance, particularly that arranged at Dingwall Motor auctions in Croydon, and he brought much of that business with him. His interest in aviation, together with the new location, inspired the move into aircraft insurance. This side of the business is the fastest growing and Jennings & Company are the only insurance brokers to be corporate members of the Royal Aero Club. Interestingly, Molly Jones, the sister of Amy Johnson, the famous record breaking pilot of the 1930s, visited the offices at the airport during the company's time there and Norman Pocock maintained contact with her until her death in 1996.

In 1976, Jennings & Company became totally independent once more, when Mr Pocock bought it on the retirement of Mr Haigh. It continues to offer advice on all personal and commercial insurance and is proud to support only insurers operating in the UK authorised by the Department of Trade and Industry, for their customers' complete security.

Top: *Airport control tower - occupied by Jennings' offices (circa 1977).* ***Left:*** *Norman Pocock (left) providing an ad hoc conducted tour of the control tower to an aviation enthusiast (circa 1977).*

It's the service that counts

Left: 115 Addiscombe Road in the early 1900s. ***Below:*** *The same building in the 1930s.*

changing but many car owners, who walked to work or used public transport, regarded their motors as existing purely for summer outings. As their cars were lifted on blocks for the winter and the wheels removed and wrapped to prevent damage to the tyres part of Leo Dove's custom was seasonal.

On leaving the Army in 1918 Leo Dove served his five year apprenticeship at the Austin Motor Company's Longbridge works outside Birmingham. From there he worked for eighteen months as a salesman with the Hans Crescent Motor Co., in one of the smarter parts of Knightsbridge in London. By 1925 he was ready to run his own show in Russell Road, Wimbledon, not far from the open spaces of Wimbledon Common.

It was here that his Wimbledon Central Motor Company established a reputation for good workmanship and honesty that was to enable him to expand throughout the South East. In those early days cars were still regarded as a rich man's toy as the style and degree of comfort in famous British marques reflected this belief. Attitudes were

Things were changing as the craze for affordable two seaters swept the country and opened motoring to a wider public. As a result Leo Dove opened a second garage at Addiscombe Road in Croydon, trading as L F Dove Ltd. Both establishments sold new and second hand cars, and petrol too from the hand operated pumps which had replaced the business of pouring petrol from cans through funnels into the cars. Other garages services such as crankshaft grinding and repairs to big ends and main bearings reflected the skills of a Longbridge trained apprentice over the blacksmiths who had taken on motor repair work. L S Dove Ltd were awarded the main dealership for Austin Cars and Commercials for Croydon and Jaguar Standard and Austin at Wimbledon.

During the second world war, when private cars went out of use, the business was kept alive by contracts to repair military searchlights and their generators. Some of the workshops were made over to manufacturing tank turrets which enabled the firm to retain a nucleus of skilled men who would have otherwise been called up. Motoring became a British passion after the war and this brought about the changes in public transport so the business run by Leo Dove, and his twin sons Geoffrey and David, expanded to include branches in Andover, Fareham and Woking to the west, Bognor Regis and Folkestone on the coast, and Ashford, Borough Green and Canterbury to the east.

Control of the company evolved to Geoffrey and David following their father's death in 1957. Since then they have diversified into finance and trucks, engineering and contract hire and even into the popular leisure field of dry ski slopes. In 1965 the Dove Group bought out the South Croydon Austin dealers Milne and Russell from Monty Duck. Ten years later Dove's celebrated their Golden Anniversary by acquiring Peacocks Ltd, the Ford dealers in Folkestone. In 1985 the Croydon business, except the Jaguar agency, was sold to Tristar Motors. Doves then won contracts with the Chrysler Jeep

Company, USA, and Saab of Sweden in 1993. The Dove tradition of employing factory trained mechanics continued to provide customers with the highest level of service in all departments. Most of the Dove branches have been awarded the ISO 9002 accreditation in recognition of the standards achieved.

When the giant 400 year old Sumitomo Corporation of Japan sought to expand into the British market they naturally chose the Dove Group as a kindred spirit to the Sumitomo Corporation business principles.

Since then the renamed Summit Group have further strengthened their partnership with Ford Motor Company by purchasing the Invicta Group based in Canterbury, and the Dees Group in Croydon and City Ford Wimbledon now renamed Dees of Wimbledon.

However the Head Office is still based in Croydon and the trade names Doves and Dees continue to flourish and benefit from their close links in the Croydon area.

Top: Austin House, 98 Lower Addiscombe Road in 1957. **Below:** The new Dove showroom at 115 Addiscombe Road in 1963.

At the forefront of Croydon's furniture trade

It would be hard to imagine a home in Croydon that did not have a piece of furniture that had made its way through the doors of Reeves. So well known is the business, that you do not have to know the address to find it. Ask a local where Church Street is and she will think for a moment and then give you the right directions. But ask her the way to Reeves' Corner and the answer will be with you in a flash. That part of Croydon was known by the family business name for donkeys' years. So much so, that when the road system in the area was changed in 1977, Reeves' Corner became the official name and postal address.

The present chief executives, Trevor and Graham Reeves, are the great-great grandsons of the founder of the company, Edwin Reeves. A sixth generation, Trevor's daughter, Natasha, keeps dad up to scratch as she works in the office. When old Edwin came to

Croydon from Sherbourne, in Dorset, it was half way through the reign of Queen Victoria. The Crimean War had finished, the Americans had just finished their Civil War and the age of the Industrial Revolution was in full swing. It was 1867. The shop front he began to trade from only measured 35 ft in length; compare that with the many hundreds of feet it takes up to-day. Edwin was a barrel maker and it was in that trade that he made his start in Croydon. Helped by his wife and brother, he branched out along other avenues. Ironmongery became one of the first new aspects of the business to be added. Before long, the famous Reeves' connection with furniture was made. As the sales grew, it was one of his four sons, William Arthur, who helped the physical growth of the shop itself. He took charge in

Left: *Edwin Reeves with his wife and colleagues outside the premises.* **Below:** *The 1920s fleet.* **Bottom:** *The shop in the 1960s.*

The war meant that all manufacturing had to be devoted to the war effort, so good quality used stock was at a premium. In 1947, the firm became E Reeves Ltd. As a limited company, it was William's son, William Thomas, who became its managing director. He carried on at the helm until his death at the ripe old age of 82. He was succeeded by his son, Maurice, the father of Trevor and Graham. They have strong sporting connections in the area. Maurice was a cricketer of some note and his interest in motor sport was inherited by Trevor, who was a rally-cross and circuit racing champion. Graham reserved his talents for the golf course, where he is a formidable opponent.

Nowadays, E Reeves Ltd concentrates on the sale of new furniture. Holding such large stocks, it can supply most, if not all, a customer's needs straight away. There is none of this nonsense about waiting weeks for a delivery, as you get with some companies. It is this speedy and efficient service that has kept the Reeves' store not just at the corner, but at the forefront of the furniture trade in Croydon. With a new livery for the millennium and the recently completed Croydon Tramlink service, the House of Reeves, the company's new trading name, is set to carry on the quality and tradition of the past generations for years to come.

Left: The 1960s fleet. **Top:** Reeves in Crown Hill. **Below:** The first Croydon Tramlink tram going past the shop.

1913. Ye Olde Curiositie Shoppe, as it was known, took over several neighbouring properties during the Great War and, by 1917, an auction room had been added, along with showrooms for second-hand furniture. The business went from strength to strength and other branches were opened. One was in Sherbourne, from where William's father had come half a century before. Another site in Croydon and one in Caterham gave opportunity to sell timber and building materials, so widening the scope of the firm.

The first auctions were held at Church Street in 1917 and by November, 1937 exactly 1,000 had been held. The last one took place in 1985. During World War II, a good trade in second-hand furniture was carried on.

Surrey's best kept secret

Nestling in 205 acres of secluded parkland overlooking the Surrey Downs, it is quite understandable that some Surrey residents may not be aware of the Selsdon Park Hotel, a fine neo-Jacobean mansion which boasts a history spanning over one thousand years.

The first recorded existence of a mansion on the present site, somewhat meagre by today's standards, was in the time of Alfred the Great. The history of the house is recorded in the Doomsday book and is linked to royalty and the Order of the Knights of Templar - better known for their courageous pursuits in the Crusades.

In 1540, Sir John Gresham became the first Lord of the Manor and in 1670, at the time of the restoration in the reign of Charles II, a new farmhouse was built which forms the core of the present architecture. At the end of the eighteenth century most of the building was demolished, with the exception of this farmhouse, to create a new and illustrious country residence - a magnificent example of nineteenth century gothic style architecture. Under the ownership of the Sanderson family, who acquired the property in 1923, the building was spectacularly enlarged. The original building was encased in red brick and today it spans a total of 640 feet. The golf course was designed and introduced to the site in 1929 by JH Taylor - Golf Open Champion.

The Hotel's undulating acres feature resplendent woodlands and graduated terraces. There are two cedars (one 400 years old, the other over 250) and a Lebanon cedar tree planted by Queen Elizabeth I.

Noted in 1799 "Remarkable not only for the salubrity of the air and beauty of its scenery... but likewise for its seeming seclusion from the bustle of country towns", this description of Selsdon Park is remarkably apt today.

Above: Mr Wickham Noakes and shooting party outside Selsdon House in 1903. Below: The present day frontage of Selsdon Park Hotel.

Today's management and staff invite clients to experience the elegance and charm of one of the most distinctive country hotels in the South of England. Situated on the edge of the cosmopolitan capital and within easy reach of the international airports of London Gatwick and London Heathrow, Selsdon Park Hotel is an oasis of peace and tranquillity.

Since being acquired by Principal Hotels in 1997, the thoughtfully planned £2.5 million refurbishment has succeeded in rendering Selsdon Park a distinctive, period hotel which embodies an appreciative blending of the old and the new. Polished wood panelling combine with rich colour schemes and fabrics to provide a uniquely eloquent, yet comfortable feel. Each of the 204 bedrooms has four star deluxe facilities, many with captivating views of the golf course and surrounding countryside. An idyllic setting for celebrating every type of social occasion, Selsdon Park Hotel can provide personalised catering for all events, from private dinner parties and formal banquets to the most memorable wedding reception. The hotel also boasts 27 meeting rooms, catering from two to four hundred delegates and has two state-of-the-art Motivator rooms with interactive walls. Excellent cuisine, complemented by a fine choice of wines, will surpass even the highest expectations. The Cedar Restaurant has achieved two Rosette Awards, is fully air conditioned and overlooks the terraces and gardens. Fine dining comprises menus with truly international style. Alternatively, the Phoenix Grill offers a more informal atmosphere.

For the more energetic guest, the hotel provides a variety of outdoor sporting pursuits including golf, jogging trail, croquet, tennis and outdoor swimming pool. The first class indoor leisure club facilities encompass an indoor swimming pool, mini-gym, sauna, solarium, steam room, squash courts and beauty treatment rooms.

So... why not discover the secret of Selsdon Park Hotel: the superb blend of old tradition and history, combined with all the modern benefits of a superb four star deluxe country house hotel?

Above: *A view of the Hotel from the rolling grounds.*
Top: *The Cedar Restaurant.*

The eyes have had it for over a century

If you are squinting to read this, then you are in good company. Some 60 percent of the population wear glasses or contact lenses. Rawlings has been offering its clients good and consistent eyecare in and around Croydon for over 100 years. The experienced and professional staff help customers choose the best product for their needs and their purses. In that way, satisfaction is guaranteed, as value for money is not measured just in the cost of the frame. The personal touch and a good after sales service are difficult to measure, but are an invaluable part of what Rawlings has to offer.

The family firm, going back four generations, began life at North End, Croydon in 1895. Alfred J Rawling opened his shop as a combination of the jewellery, watchmaking and optical trades. As a child, times had been hard. It was no fun in the Victorian era to be one of five children brought up by a widowed mother. It gave him a determination to succeed and make his own mark on life. He was still in his 20s when he banked his first day's takings. The princely sum of six shillings (30p) was the total in the till. Although apprenticed to his uncle as a jeweller and watchmaker, it was in the optical side of his own business that he showed a special interest. Whilst still working in the shop, he trained as an optician and passed the examinations of the Worshipful Company of Spectacle Makers in 1904. That diploma still has pride of place on the wall at Rawling & Oldfield on High Street, Croydon. The back rooms of the shop were used as consulting rooms, whilst an assistant ran the other business interests from the front. His wife, Hilda, gave birth to five children. The four boys all became ophthalmic opticians and the daughter, Ruth, was the book keeper for 30 years.

The business expanded and successive generations have all been involved in this growth. Branches opened in Purley, Caterham, Maidstone, Winchester and Alton, to name but a few. By the end of the 20th century, ten such Rawlings, as it is now known, can be found.

Above left: *Alfred Rawling, founder of the firm.*
Below: *The original shop in the early years of the 20th century.*

By kind permission of the Croydon Advertiser Group

Reginald Foort was a well known organist of the 1930s, and Croydon was privileged to welcome the famous man to play at the Empire in North End. Foort came prepared; he brought with him his 'portable' organ - a description that today would contravene the Trades Descriptions Act. The impressive instrument was built in the USA by the firm Moller especially for touring, though the organ needed no fewer than seven large vans to transport it from place to place! Attracted by the drama of the moment, a small crowd has gathered to watch Pickfords - an old name in the town - deliver the organ to the theatre. Foort's organ was only the second five-manual organ in the country; the other was resident at the Odeon in Leicester Square. After touring the country for two years the organ was taken over by the BBC at the outbreak of World War II.

John Gent

John Gent - Editorial consultant

John was born in South Norwood and has always lived in the Croydon area. He attended Cypress Road and Selhurst Grammar schools and took a keen interest in local history from the age of about 15. After National Service in the Royal Air Force he joined the staff of London Transport where he worked for 38 years. He decided to retire early so as to devote more time to his interests which include collecting postcards, transport, model railways, travel, walking, photography, writing, and gardens.

He has been President of the Croydon Natural History & Scientific Society three times, is a Vice President, and was founder Chairman of the Croydon Society, and has for many years been a member of the Surrey Local History Council. John has been involved in editing or writing ten books, mainly of local interest to Croydon, and has written numerous articles. He lectures extensively and over the years has built up a large collection of photographs, both old and recent, because, as he says, "History did not just happen yesterday. We are part of it and it is important that we should leave a record of today's surroundings and events for the future."

John can remember the trolleybuses being introduced in 1936, when his Grandfather took him for a ride to the Crystal Palace. His recollections of wartime Croydon are very vivid and 22 flying bombs, or "Doodle Bugs" fell within a mile of his home, causing much damage. He watched the various parades depicted on pages 48 to 51, saw the last tram in 1951, the last trolleybus in 1960 and looks forward to riding on Croydon's new trams in the new millenium. Yes, he was in the audience on the last night at the Grand in 1959 (page 26)!

Bibliography

Croydon Between the Wars - Croydon Natural History & Scientific Society Ltd

Croydon in the 1940s and 1950s - Croydon Natural History & Scientific Society Ltd

Croydon Airport - Mike Hooks

The People's War - Juliet Gardiner

A police officer has been drafted in to help pedestrians cross near the old Public Hall in George Street in a scene from the 1950s.

Acknowledgments

Special thanks are due to the following people for their contribution to the book:
Mr Malcolm J. Starbrook, Editor of the Croydon Advertiser Group. The Croydon Advertiser Group kindly granted permission to reproduce eight of their photographs held in Croydon Local Studies Library and we are very grateful for that. Mr John Gent for the loan of several images and his wealth of local knowledge, kindness and enthusiasm for the project. Mrs Heather G. Kirby, Stephen Griffiths and their colleagues at Croydon Local Studies Library for their generous permission to reproduce images from their lovely collection. Mrs Tracey Jacques at Chorley Handford Ltd. Last, but not least, Mrs Salvina Bartholomeusz and Ms Jacquie Gomm of Allders for their patient assistance in supplying photographs from the store's archives.

Thanks are also due to
Peggy Burns who penned the editorial text and
Margaret Wakefield and Andrew Mitchell for their copywriting skills

Peggy Burns has written many history books, including the Stepping Through History series for Wayland.
She also holds a Childrens' Book of the Year Award (1988)